Wanna F*ck?

Wanna F*ck?

Bel Olid

Translated from Catalan
by Laura McGloughlin

With illustrations by Glòria Vives

polity

Originally published in Catalan as *Follem?* by Bridge. Copyright © Bel Olid, 2018. Rights negotiated and controlled by Asterisc Agents.

This English translation © Polity Press, 2025.

The translation of this work has been supported by the Institut Ramon Llull.

Polity Press
65 Bridge Street
Cambridge CB2 1UR, UK

Polity Press
111 River Street
Hoboken, NJ 07030, USA

All rights reserved. Except for the quotation of short passages for the purpose of criticism and review, no part of this publication may be reproduced, stored in a retrieval system or transmitted, in any form or by any means, electronic, mechanical, photocopying, recording or otherwise, without the prior permission of the publisher.

ISBN-13: 978-1-5095-6475-0 (hardback)
ISBN-13: 978-1-5095-6476-7 (paperback)

A catalogue record for this book is available from the British Library.

Library of Congress Control Number: 2024951698

Typeset in 11.5 on 14pt Adobe Garamond Pro
by Cheshire Typesetting Ltd, Cuddington, Cheshire
Printed and bound in Great Britain by CPI Group (UK) Ltd, Croydon

The publisher has used its best endeavours to ensure that the URLs for external websites referred to in this book are correct and active at the time of going to press. However, the publisher has no responsibility for the websites and can make no guarantee that a site will remain live or that the content is or will remain appropriate.

Every effort has been made to trace all copyright holders, but if any have been overlooked the publisher will be pleased to include any necessary credits in any subsequent reprint or edition.

For further information on Polity, visit our website:
politybooks.com

To us: let's turn
the battlefield
into a party.

Contents

~~map~~
penknife
page 1

~~sex~~
sexualities
page 5

~~LGBTIQ~~
life
page 13

~~foreplay~~
fucking
page 29

~~consent~~
enthusiasm
page 51

~~beauty~~
expectations
page 71

~~vibrator~~
toys
page 87

~~sex education~~
care
page 97

~~love~~
affection
page 109

~~end~~
horizon
page 121

**appendix:
how d'you wanna fuck?**
page 123

~~map~~ penknife

If sexuality was a planet, this book wouldn't claim to be a map. More a penknife. A penknife can anticipate some of the situations you might find yourself in when you go out exploring, but it's particularly useful because it offers versatile tools to help you in unforeseen situations. The engineer who designed the tin opener feature thought about the fact that you'd need to open a tin. But you can use it to scratch your back, clean under your nails, measure stuff, and for a thousand other things that don't come to mind because I'm not really one for hiking and I've never had a penknife.

Sexuality as a planet, then (and sexualities as a universe), but not an unknown planet we reach at puberty, or even when we become adults. Foetuses in the womb can already be seen persistently touching their genitals. It's normal to see five-year-old cis girls in junior school looking for the best way to rub their crotch against a cushion, small groups playing 'mummies and daddies', two friends looking at each other and touching each other. The older they get, the more they hide. We learn quickly that sexuality (I prefer to speak of it in the plural, but we'll talk about that later) is a private matter which must be hidden. And yet, we're constantly bombarded with images, songs, jokes that refer to it.

There are many rules and they're learned without anyone explicitly spelling them out. In our culture, we can show our nose and elbows, but not our genitals. Nor can women show their breasts (except at the beach). We can scratch our ears in public, but not our genitals. We can kiss each other on the mouth as part of a couple (especially if it's a heterosexual one), but not if there are more than two of us. You can caress someone else's thigh in public up to a point, but you must never reach the genitals. The message is basically 'dirty genitals'. Instead of happy genitals, lively genitals, pleasurable genitals, hooray for genitals.

On the other hand, such obsession with genitalia desexualizes the rest of the body. We end up believing that genitals are the only source of sexual pleasure, precisely because sexual pleasure is private and we can show and touch everything else in public without sanction.

So, this penknife wants to be used not only as a tool for dealing with unexpected situations (and expected ones too, if you also need to open a tin from time to time) but especially as a weapon for dismantling all that we've been taught about sex: what it means, how to do it and how not to do it.

Because perhaps the first thing we have to learn about sex is to unlearn. Unlearn the desire we've been taught we should feel, unlearn the shame. Forget the bodies we've been obliged to like, forget the activities perceived as the only options. Wipe the images of commercial pornography from your mind; forget the role that's fallen to us to play.

And then with fresh eyes, look deep inside and ask ourselves what we want, what we like, what we feel like discovering. And look outward, too. Look at everything in front of us, not automatically rejecting anything. Listen to our desire, and when we know what we want, listen to the other person and learn what they want and whether the two are compatible. Dare ourselves to hesitate, explore, make mistakes, stop at any time. Dare ourselves to break out of 'what should be' and immerse ourselves in what makes us tingle.

In this way, the penknife this book wants to be has a special tool: a screwdriver dreamed up to dismantle everything of no use to us. And to build a boat that can carry us to a paradise we might not yet know exists.

However, the knife comes with some limitations that are the engineer's fault. It's made from materials tried and tested in specific personal circumstances, over forty years of trial and error – and some wise decisions. The engineer is a non-binary person, less cis passing every day, in a more or less normative body that doesn't give them too much trouble. The engineer desires a wide variety of bodies and has suffered several assaults. The engineer is a happily rebellious, intensely sexual feminist. The engineer is Western, white, a compulsive reader. The engineer doesn't know much about a lot of things in life.

Luckily, it's not the only knife or the only material or the only tool you'll find for dismantling clichés and building yourselves a friendly sexuality to live in. Luckily, it is only a drop in the ocean, and the clouds raining on us are as diverse as life itself. Let's add it to the sea of the possible.

~~sex~~ sexualities

There is a space between our legs that we hide, like a secret or a treasure or a prison sentence. We hide it but it has a weight, a symbolic presence even though it can't be seen. It's not like eyes or hands, in plain sight. No one knows for sure what we have there, between our legs, but they imagine. They look at our long hair or our beard and assume, as if a woman without a vulva or a penis without a man doesn't exist. This treasure, this secret, determines our lives, determines what box we're put in, what we're expected to do and not do. It's so important that we hide it, we cover it, we worship it, we hate it. One possible meaning of sex is precisely that mysterious land of the external sex organs; another would be *sexuality*, an even more mysterious, even more complex concept.

If you ask any fifteen-year-old what questions they have about sex, it's possible that they'll laugh and say they have none. We have information, films, examples within reach in quantities unthinkable thirty years ago. Even so, this avalanche of data and images is exactly what makes us take it for granted that there's nothing more to be discovered. We accept clichés as indisputable facts and when what we feel doesn't fit with what we're told *we should feel*, we question ourselves rather than the beliefs that deny us the possibility of existing.

What is simply cultural is *normalized* and the idea of normality, of inflexible options, is imposed even where diversity is more common. For this reason, I prefer to speak of *sexualities* rather than *sex*: sexualities as plural, personal, adaptable ways of experiencing sex and everything that comes with it.

The fact that genitals are at the centre of the dominant sexuality hugely complicates our lives. This will crop up repeatedly and be considered from all angles, but it's worth pointing it out from the start. On one hand, placing the entire burden of sexuality on genitals prevents us from seeing that it's possible to feel sexual pleasure in zones of the body that aren't seen socially as *sexual*, and, at the same time, turns genitals into this kind of sacred totem, a supreme symbol that enslaves us. On the other, splitting society into two supposedly unique, inescapable, opposing and complementary biological sexes has led to the idea that heterosexuality is the norm, and created a binary system of genders which causes enormous inequalities.

This system is sustained by the lie saying that all people can be divided into two groups (at least biologically): men and women. When you're born, they examine your genitals and you're labelled as a member of one of the groups. Seems easy, right? Indisputable. Every school teaches that boys have a penis and girls a vulva. However, it turns out that in 1 in every 1,500 births (according to the Intersex Society of North America), there is someone who is harder to classify. In fact, it's so difficult that a team of experts in sexual differentiation has to weigh in on the case. Looking between their legs is no longer enough; chromosomal and hormonal tests are required to dispel the uncertainty about what are medically termed *ambiguous genitalia*.

They'll look at the chromosomes. Again, we've got it into our heads that there are XX (women) and XY (men) people and therefore testing will immediately clear things up. Another lie. There are other possibilities: for example, 0.1 per cent of the population has XXY chromosomes. The other marker of what is called *biological sex* are hormones: which we produce and how we process them. We're not told about the greater diversity here either. If you want to know more, you can look into the *SRY* and *DMRT1* genes and their role in what is called *biological sex*.

It's calculated that close to 1 per cent of the population doesn't physically fit (when it comes to genitals, chromosomes or hormones) in either of the two categories that have been sold to us as the only ones. The group of people (among whom there is huge variance) belonging to this 1 per cent is called *intersex* – that is, *between the sexes*. It's a large category (in Barcelona, which has a population of one and a half million people, there are more than 15,000 intersex people; in a school with two classes in each year group, an intersex person will enrol every two years).

Some of these people undergo surgical intervention when they are only a few months old to make them conform to the norm. This can cause sterility or block the ability to experience certain types of pleasure. As a first step, intersex advocacy organizations ask for there to be no surgical intervention for something that isn't a medical problem, but natural (and very common) variation. They call for intersex people to be the ones to decide, when they have the capacity to do so, whether or not they wish to subject themselves to surgeries – which, far from improving their health, can actually make it worse. They also fight for a separate box in official documentation, so they don't need to tick 'man' or 'woman' if they don't want to.

This struggle, which we should support as a simple question of human rights, also paves the way for questioning what has been sold to us as *scientific fact*. It turns out that science is undertaken by people with ideologies, and some of them are ready to despise a significant section of the population if it clashes with their ideology.

If our whole system of sexes is a social construct and not scientific fact, which means our lives are based on a lie, how can we trust what we're told about sexuality? I look at my body, and recognize the basic form of what I've been told belongs to a woman. Specifically, a cis woman. But as I've learned how it works, as I've given up modifying it in certain ways (by shaving or wearing bras, for example), and begun modifying it in others (with tattoos or binders, for example), as I've been dressing less and less how I'm supposed to dress, my appearance has begun to move away from the solidified hegemonies of what a woman should be, and begun to approach an ever more blurred frontier.

The body carries a specific weight in sexuality: we experience it through the body. But the body isn't disconnected from beliefs. Quite the opposite: we can condition it to feel or not feel certain things, in a kind of Pavlov effect. Our desire is definitely affected by what we believe we *should desire*. But it's not only desire – it's also the pleasure we allow ourselves to feel, or try not to feel because we're ashamed or surprised by it.

So the most difficult task we face in order to enjoy sexuality in general, and our own in particular, is to listen to our bodies, leaving prejudice aside as much as we can. Try to unlock the desires we've been told are unacceptable and see where they lead us. We've constructed the cathedral of normality on the lie of biology, still bearing the hallmark of what is natural, and established a catalogue of acceptable identities, desires and practices. We see them portrayed everywhere – explicitly in pornography and implicitly in all forms of culture. There is a paradox in the fact that we condemn respectful sexualities where no one is forced while we normalize rape and child abuse through stories that objectify women and sexualize children.

This *normality*, expressed both passively and actively in our daily lives, isolates us when what we feel doesn't conform to it. Sometimes we think we're the only ones who feel as we feel, who like what we like. If it's already hard to listen to yourself and identify your own desire, it's even harder when it doesn't match the norm.

Here I'm in no way suggesting that any old sexuality is fine: sexualities that rest on oppression of any kind are unacceptable. Any sexual practice must begin from the principle that everyone participating does so freely: that is, they must be able to weigh up its risks and benefits, and also genuinely able to refuse if they don't want to participate.

The clearest example is that of children and young people, who clearly have a sexual life, but one that has to be experienced between equals. Involving minors in adult sexual practices is not only an offence, it's also a crime that assaults their emotional and sexual development. There can also be inequalities between adults, but we'll discuss this extensively in the chapter about consent/enthusiasm.

We create a happy sexuality by first listening to ourselves, but it's also essential to listen to the people we have sex with. And to open ourselves to setting out on the exciting road of discovering the less travelled paths of our bodies, of our desire. Revealing the secret, sharing the treasure, freeing ourselves from disapproval.

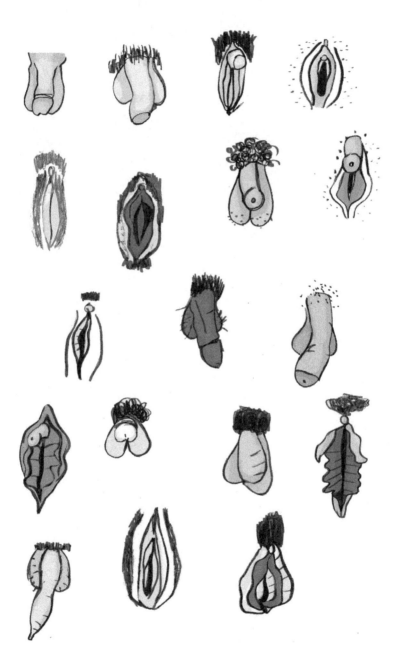

~~LGBTIQ+~~ life

If we've been able to convert as tangible a thing as the body into a tangled labyrinth of lies, what won't we do with the ethereal force of desire? We've simplified it, we've carved it up, we've mutilated it, we've robbed it of meaning, we've denied it. We've hounded it, we've blinded it, tamed it, deadened it. And, when it's gone off-script, we've demonized, shrunk, persecuted it. In the process of diminishing the unattainable, we've created labels that claim to classify us as *normal* people and *strange* people.

Lesbians, bisexuals, gays, trans, intersex, queer and more. This alphabet soup, which keeps gaining acronyms as we uncover oppressions we'd normalized until now, is a curious blend of sexual orientations, gender identities, gender expressions and even non-normative biological sexes. But, before we go any further, let's unpack a little what all of this means.

Naming ourselves so we exist

Biological sex relates to certain physical characteristics we're born with and how they are interpreted. Even though officially we can only be registered as *woman* or *man*, there are actually women, men and intersex people. You're assigned a gender according to your biological sex. Right now in our society, we're assigned only as a woman or a man, rather than giving a person the chance to express their preference for one group or the other. Because of this, intersex people are subjected to operations or other medical procedures which 'adjust' their bodies as far as possible to the social demands of what a woman's or man's body means, in order to assign them to one of the two normative genders. Different behaviours are expected of the people assigned to each gender, and we condition little ones to follow the gender mandate – the rules imposed on us according to whether we've been classified as future women or future men, and which will push us to develop certain gender roles.

On the other hand, there is gender identity, our internal perception of the gender to which we belong, which doesn't always coincide with the gender assigned to us at birth. Here the fan unfolds: in addition to 'woman' and 'man', we have various gender identities, such as gender fluid (a dynamic mix of man and woman, with moments in which one carries more weight than the other) or agender (not a man or a woman). There are also people who identify as non-binary or gender-neutral (outside the system of genders), and a thousand other labels that we often group under the queer umbrella (which goes beyond gender identity, but also includes it).

The people who have a gender identity that coincides with the gender they were assigned at birth are cisgender or cis people. Those who don't are trans people, because they *transition* from one gender to another. This transition can be between the two normative genders or towards being non-binary, and can involve body modifications (via hormonal treatments, surgeries or prostheses) or not. Some people who fall outside the binary don't identify as trans, some don't identify as cis.

Gender expression is how we represent the gender we identify with in society. Normative gender expressions are those that stick to social norms. For example, a woman who wears her hair long, dresses in clothes and accessories bought from the women's section in shops, removes her body hair, wears make-up, and uses gestures traditionally considered feminine, has a normative gender expression, because she's a woman that looks like a woman (according to social demands). Anything else is a non-normative expression of gender. We very often assume that a person with a non-normative gender expression also has a non-normative sexual orientation, even though they don't necessarily go together.

Sexual orientation is about what kind of person attracts us, whether sexually, emotionally, romantically, spiritually . . . We label sexual orientation according to the relationship between the gender of the person desiring and the genders of the people desired. When a person feels attracted to people of their own gender, they're considered homosexual, and if they feel attracted to people of the other gender, they're considered heterosexual. If they're attracted to people of both their own gender and the other, they're bisexual.

This classification comes up against an obvious stumbling-block: it rests on the binary conception of gender (as if there were only two) when we've spent the last few pages trying to make it clear that *there are more than two genders* (and also more than two sexes). To avoid this pitfall, some people state that the 'bisexual' label encompasses attraction to all genders, and others label themselves pansexuals: those who feel attracted to people of various genders. On the other hand, asexual people don't feel sexually attracted to anyone. Among asexual people, there are those who don't feel sexual attraction but do feel emotional attraction, and those who don't feel either. There are also people who can feel sexual attraction at certain times, but in an exceptional, short-lived way, and they call themselves asexual too. Some masturbate (they don't feel attraction for other people, but they do have a desire for solitary sexual pleasure);

others don't. Asexuality has nothing to do with celibacy, which is the conscious decision not to take part in sexual activities even if they are desired. There are also demisexual people who only feel sexual attraction to people with whom they have strong emotional bonds, and feel no sexual attraction for people they don't know or with whom they don't have a loving or trusting relationship.

Note that with all orientations (except asexuality and demisexuality), we talk about attraction according to gender, but there are other aspects that also come into play. For example, we might be attracted to people with specific expressions of gender, or with specific physical characteristics. Or who like the same music as us, or taking photos of butterflies. There are names for all this (and much more) too, but we won't get into it. The difference is that there's no discrimination against people who desire people with short hair, for example. There's only discrimination if they are (or seem to be) of the same gender.

What use are they really, these labels? And once we've found one that fits, does that mean it won't change? If reality isn't monosexual and the majority of people have felt attraction to people of different genders at some point in their lives, wouldn't it be easier to simply erase all the labels and go with what we feel at a given moment? In the world I'd like to live in, yes. In the world I actually live in, it's a little more complicated.

Go forth and multiply

The Christian tradition that permeates Western culture tries to persuade us that sex has nothing to do with desire, only with reproduction. Desire is an evil that, if it can't be avoided, must be prevented from controlling what we do. As long as they could reproduce without feeling desire, people who have a vulva and have been raised to be women were excluded from the fairground of recreational sexuality.

It's not been that way for years now, you'll say. And you'd be right. Since the development of effective, accessible contraception that doesn't depend on the collaboration of cis men, women have been freed from procreation as a probable consequence of cisheterosexual – or cishet, for short – relations, and therefore been able to explore their sexuality with less fear. At the same time, this ideology is the basis for certain beliefs that have taken root so deeply in the collective consciousness that they still stain the glass through which we view non-reproductive sexualities.

To start with, the (false, as we've already seen) separation into just two groups of people, men and women, serves the reproductive vision of sexuality: to reproduce, at least two fertile people with differing reproductive organs are required. If we equate sexuality with reproduction, the default combination is cis man and cis woman. That is, cishet sexuality. People who follow reproductive logic are the 'normal' ones, even when their sexual activities don't have this aim. From birth, we are spoon-fed the idea that we must find a partner to reproduce with, and for many people it's a virtually never-ending source of unhappiness.

We grow up without anyone explicitly telling us we must be heterosexual, but with a thousand messages indicating that there is no other option. We ask little girls if they have a boyfriend, and little boys if they have a girlfriend; in stories and films, we only show them heterosexual couples. This is perhaps beginning to change, in the sense that the media are starting to show couples (always couples – this we don't question) of two men and two women. At the same time, the implication is that this is an exception to the rule, and these representations also present homosexuality as acceptable only in as far as the other norms are obeyed: monogamy and the will to 'create a family'.

I remember myself at fifteen, looking at my maths teacher's breasts (a stunning woman) and my language teacher's bum (a stunning man), thinking that I was the only one who wasn't heterosexual or homosexual in the school and probably the universe. I'd never heard the terms *monosexual*, *bisexual* or *pansexual* then, and the only homosexuals ever mentioned were men. I was a victim of the presumption of heterosexuality – that is, the idea that everyone who doesn't say different is heterosexual – and also of the erasure of lesbians, whose existence people will deny until they're blue in the face. Compulsory heterosexuality is a closet we are all placed in at birth and those of us who fit in there are comfortable; people who identify as heterosexuals never have to come out of it – only those who desire in a non-normative way do.

Coming out of the closet?
Coming out of the closet isn't something you do one day of your life and that's that – from then on, you can live happy and free. Every time you walk down the street with someone you have a romantic and sexual relationship with and you feel like kissing them, you have to decide whether it's a safe environment or not, because until you kiss them you're protected (and oppressed in equal measure) by the presumption of heterosexuality. Every time you start a new job, every time you meet someone new, you have to decide whether to continue 'pretending' or to clearly express your non-normative orientation or identity. Trans people are ejected from the closet, whether they want to be or not, every time they have to show official documents on which sex or birth name are mentioned (and until not long ago it was extremely difficult to change official documentation). Bisexual or pansexual people, on the other hand, are read as heterosexuals when they have a partner of the other majority gender, and as homosexuals when they

have a partner of their own gender. This means being rendered even more invisible than lesbians are, which is already brutal enough.

Coming out of the closet should always be a personal decision: no one has the right to pull you out. We're exercising a form of violence when we reveal the non-normative sexuality of someone we know. A person telling you that they're not cishet doesn't mean they give you permission to tell the rest of humanity. In the same way, maybe you think a person you know who is living as a heterosexual perhaps isn't. Making jokes about their presumed non-heterosexuality can harm them. We can bring the subject up by talking about our own experience, but it's better to let the other person express themselves without interrogation about what they like or what they don't.

Desiring, existing
Part of the burden of gender that falls on women is specifically not being subjects of their own desire: they are raised to be

desired *by men*, not to desire others. But they feel very vivid desire, very different from how they've been made to believe it should be. Some decide that not having a name for that reality is neither here nor there; they live it and enjoy it. However, for many it takes years to shake off the preconceptions about what their sexuality should be, and to truly listen to what their body wants from them.

Labels are useful because, in a world where *it is assumed* that the vast majority of people is cishet, the fact that there are ways of naming other realities opens the door to the possibility of simply being ourselves. If progressive sex ed had been around before I'd reached the age of fifteen, I wouldn't have had to think twice when I found myself attracted to people of the gender I'd been assigned, nor would I have confused sexual attraction with 'womance' for so long. I had to identify the feelings I was having as sexual desire, which at the beginning isn't as easy as it seems, and admit it as a possibility. Cishet people don't have to go through this process, because all of society takes for granted that at some point in life you will feel desire, and it will be for people of the 'other' gender (and you're not expected to maintain close friendships with them either).

I'm sure that there were many other people at school who were experiencing similar things to me. Why didn't we talk about them? For fear of rejection, discrimination, the humiliations that at some time or other we've all witnessed being experienced by people who deviate from the norm in a *conspicuous way*. Stressing 'conspicuous' is important. We don't discriminate against people for what they are, but for what they seem to be. Because of this, we assume that people with non-normative gender expressions must have non-normative sexual orientations too, to the point that *butch* or *fag*, which were first used to insult lesbians and gays, are more likely to be assessments of gender expression than of sexual orientation. There isn't even an insult for bisexuals and pansexuals; you fall into the *dyke* or *fag* box, just as young trans women are insulted as *fags* and young trans men as *dykes*.

When you're called a *fag* they're not necessarily saying that you like men, rather that *you seem to*. You seem to because you don't express your masculine gender in a traditionally masculine way: you're therefore expelled from the *man* category, and transferred to a vague category that is *not-man* and includes all the people on the receiving end of cishet men's assertion of their right to violence.

So it goes unnoticed

Sexual orientation is easy to hide: not showing it publicly by getting too close to people of your own gender and adopting a normative expression of gender is enough. As long as you stay in the closet, you'll minimize the risk of discrimination regarding your sexual orientation. Many lesbians choose this option, because if they didn't, they would jeopardize their job, their social status, acceptance from their family, or even their lives. A recurring figure throughout the twentieth century was the 'spinster aunt' who lived with a 'female friend'. Certainly, many people imagined what was going on between the aunt and her friend, but it was accepted as long as it wasn't explicit. Even today, many lesbians introduce their partner to their family as a friend in order to avoid rejection, the cost of which can be very high.

Trans people experience an even more extreme pressure: society can come to accept that there's been an *error* in the assignation of gender at birth, and that this error can be *corrected* – but only if the transition is towards an absolutely normative expression of gender. This means obeying the gender mandate in a much stricter way than is demanded of cis people.

For example, cis women can wear their hair short or not put on make-up without any obvious discrimination against them, but in contrast, trans women who decide not to wear their hair long or put on make-up have much more difficulty in being acknowledged as women.

Some complain that many trans people decide to transition towards very traditional expressions of gender, and trans women in particular are accused of reinforcing stereotypes of gender and adopting an extreme femininity. But how can we blame them for doing so, if it's a way of suffering less discrimination? And in any case, why aren't all cis women with hyper-feminized expressions of gender similarly accused?

Dressing up

The expression of gender remains a disguise that everyone uses. Some people feel comfortable with the one which has fallen to them; others personalize it within the limits permitted. It causes others such discomfort that they break the rules to live socially in accordance with the way that they feel. But for all people, from the most comfortable to the most uncomfortable, it's a mask which can be extremely complicated (with accessories, hair removal, earrings and other body modifications) or totally functional (comfortable, neutral clothing).

Currently, there are many people who decide that they don't need to be *legible* when it comes to their gender – that is, they don't use their gender expression as a way to tell the rest of humankind what their gender identity is. There are women with beards and traditionally masculine expressions, men in low-necked tops that show their breasts, non-binary people with a binary expression. It's common for these individuals to be misgendered. It's understandable: if we don't follow traditional expressions of gender, it's more difficult for others to get it right.

One way of identifying and respecting preferences if we aren't sure is when we introduce ourselves. 'Hello, my name is Bel and I use they/them pronouns. And you?' When a person expresses a preference as to how they should be treated when it comes to gender, it's aggressive not to follow it.

Be normal

Another less obvious but equally perverse degree of discrimination is the obligation society imposes on non-cishet people to demonstrate that they are *normal* in all other aspects of their lives. You can be gay, but marry, adopt a baby, have a respectable job. In this instance, social acceptance hinges on not transgressing more than a single rule at a time – that of sexual orientation or gender identity – and following all the others in an exemplary manner.

On the other hand, there is an obsession with fixing within very rigid parameters what has been convincingly shown to be much more flexible. The Kinsey Reports, which compiled the results of a survey of more than 20,000 people conducted in the United States in the mid twentieth century, explained that very few of those surveyed were completely heterosexual or homosexual (that is, monosexual), and that a large majority moved between differing degrees of bisexuality (pansexuality, in more current parlance).

Besides, sexual orientation isn't stable. A great many people experience desire for people of various genders at different points in their lives. And that's not all: gender identity doesn't have to be fixed either. For this reason, there are more and more people who define themselves as *questioning*; they're not clear on their gender identity and/or their sexual orientation, or they feel that it's in a permanent state of flux, or they even consider divisions in gender and sexual orientation absurd.

I'll ask again: do we need to have names for everything? Yes. On one hand, because it's as if what goes unnamed doesn't exist. On the other, because if we cannot name realities which don't fit the norm, it's a lot harder for us to identify the discrimination we suffer. Labels are necessary to explain to us in detail how we desire, but also to fight against the violence suffered by those of us who aren't (and don't want to be) 'normal'.

All the same, we must remember that the only thing that people taking shelter under the LGBTQI+ acronym share is cisheterosexual oppression. The individual identity of every one of us goes beyond that alliance, and the conquest of rights such as marriage, which part of the collective has championed, hasn't been achieved for all the individuals comprising it. For example, this right isn't guaranteed for migrant lesbians who don't have the documentation the state demands. The level of protection against discrimination varies enormously depending on social status, purchasing power, exposure to aggressions such as racism, and even a person's gender. A cisgender white lesbian with a *femme* (traditionally feminine) expression suffers much less violence than a visibly trans, brown lesbian. At the same time, there are upper-class trans women, visible in public spaces (like cinema or music) who suffer less discrimination than gay, migrant, working-class cis men without papers. The collective struggle is useful to the extent that it brings up shared vulnerabilities, but it can be oppressive if it ignores individual pain and the tangles formed by various intersecting violences.

I don't think I will get to see the world I want: a world in which biological sex and gender are socially irrelevant and therefore gender expression (if there is no gender, there's no need to express it) and sexual orientation (if there are no genders, we can't label our desire according to the gender of whom we desire) disappear. It would be a world in which there'd be no need to come out of the closet, because we wouldn't be placed in there at birth. It would be a world in which wearing skirts and cutting hair would be aesthetic choices and not calling cards flagging identity to the world. It would be a world in which we'd live with our bodies as they are, and celebrate them as we please. I imagine myself meeting someone and allowing attraction to flow. That wondering what I will find under someone's clothing might be an excuse to play and discover, and not a source of anxiety or rejection. A world in which preconceived notions about what we like and what we don't disappear and leave space to explore and be surprised.

Until we get there, making the system more flexible is vital. A society in which girls who do 'boys' stuff' aren't punished, or where a boy can wear skirts and his hair long without his gender identity being questioned, is a world where more people will feel comfortable. Every comment we don't make about other people's expression of gender – especially if they are kids – brings us a little closer to the collective freedom to be who we are.

In the end, it's just about seeing the reality of the diversity of which we're made and no longer wanting to erase it. However much I think about it, I can't imagine how recognizing that we're different and ever-changing can harm anyone. And, on the contrary, being allowed to hear each other and discover each other in every moment would help so many people to be happy.

~~foreplay~~
fucking

Fucking in films
Well into the twenty-first century, films no longer end with a kiss and a fade to black. In fact, even romantic comedies usually have some kind of sex scene before the two main characters fall in love, overcome a thousand obstacles and end up happy ever after. But is the idea of sexuality (and even more so that of emotional relationships) that is fed to us by popular shows any more reliable than that suggestive first kiss?

On one hand, the vast majority of times when there is sex on screen, we see a heterosexual couple. On the other hand, coitus is always a given, even though we don't see exactly what is happening, because there are sheets, or even clothes, covering it up. The women usually don't take off their bras; it's usually enough for the men to unbutton their flies. Sometimes the act happens in a toilet or somewhere uncomfortable and it lasts less than two minutes. Very often the characters go from exchanging passionate glances to ripping their clothes off and moving to penetration (of a vagina by a penis, of course). Penises seem to enter vaginas without needing lubricant or any kind of manual aid, and very rarely does the couple decide to use a condom. After a little bit of in–out, they cry out in unison, implying they've had an orgasm. Just one,

and at the same time. Then they pull apart and sigh. Party's over.

I'm not saying it's impossible to maintain a sexual relationship like this, but any person with a little experience should recognize that it's exceptional for both parties to have an orgasm – and simultaneous ones, to boot – in such a brief interaction, with no stimulation other than coitus and with barely any communication to speak of.

The problem isn't that art is exploring exceptions, which might be interesting as a topic for reflection. The problem is when these exceptions are the only things shown and are passed off as the norm, especially when they promote expectations which are difficult to fulfil, based on a very specific type of sexual pleasure centred on the penis and coitus. That is, we've moved from the implicit 'we know what you're doing' of the fade to black to an explicit thirty-second coitus.

This hegemonic representation of sex is based on sweeping assumptions. To begin with, that sex happens between a cis man and a cis woman. Despite the whole catalogue of possible bodies, no others seem to exist. I've spoken to many heterosexual people who can't see the problem in their over-representation and argue that it shouldn't be an impediment to the rest of us being able to imagine our own sexual choices; when all is said and done, bodies aren't so important. But I don't see it quite like that. To begin with, the body is a very important part of sexuality. It's very difficult to dissociate sexuality from the body, even if we believe that many other factors come into play.

Not only that – in a society in which homophobic and transphobic comments come so easily to people, where it's always been assumed that your first crush will be on someone of the 'other gender' (because only two are envisaged), is it really just as easy to present yourself as something other than cishet?

Being heterosexual goes beyond our specific sexual practices. In fact, there are men who label themselves as heterosexuals and have sex with other men, and it's common for young women to say that what happens with their friends 'doesn't count as sex'. For these people, 'being heterosexual' is a way of life. They mean they don't see themselves as ever having a stable relationship that isn't heterosexual, and socially they *perform* as heterosexuals.

This links to a second, also erroneous and equally sweeping, idea: it's only *real* sex if there is coitus, and you only need coitus for it to be sex. When a woman who declares herself heterosexual says that she's not bisexual (and much less a lesbian!) because 'what happens between friends doesn't count as sex', she's thinking what a great many people do: two women can't fuck, because there's no penis between them. It doesn't even cross their minds that there are women who have a penis, nor do they see penetration with toys or hands, which can be very deep, as *real* penetration.

The orgasm gap

In this blow-up version of sex, it all begins when there is an erect penis and it all ends when the erection does. If deflation is because the cis penis owner's had an orgasm, it's considered complete sex. If it's for other reasons, it's considered failed sex.

Here we have a significant hurdle for enjoying sex: all studies indicate that the majority of people equipped with a clitoris reach orgasm through practices other than coitus – or in tandem with coitus – which tend to involve contact with the glans clitoris. The so-called vaginal orgasm is in fact a clitoral orgasm, in which other invisible (but very present) parts of the clitoris are stimulated.

There are a thousand jokes about the inability of certain cishet men to find the clitoris, but how many people who have one (and explore it) really know what it is? If we're asked to draw a liver, which we've never seen, we could do a more or less accurate reproduction. Even the uterus, the Fallopian tubes and ovaries are familiar. In contrast, if we were made to draw a clitoris, would we get it right? Do we know it goes far beyond the part we can see, which is only the gland? If you've never seen a single image of it, here you have one.

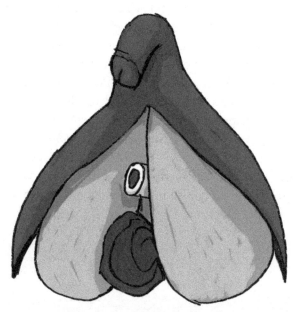

The clitoris (the entire clitoris, not just the gland) has 8,000 nerve endings (and the entire penis, not just the gland, has around 6,000). The vaginal walls, in contrast, have practically none. So it would be very difficult to reach a purely vaginal orgasm, even though it's perfectly possible to stimulate the parts of the clitoris named the *vestibular bulbs* (which surround the vaginal opening) and the *clitoral crura* through vaginal penetration. There are people who reach orgasm through stimulation only of the nipples, which also have a great many nerve endings.

Sexual pleasure is much richer than stimulation with orgasm as the goal – we'll talk more about that later – but for now we'll keep talking about this. At present, heterosexual relations with coitus are the only socially recognized sexual relations, and so it's difficult for someone with a clitoris to reach orgasm. We also know that knowledge about the scope of the clitoris is vastly inferior to our knowledge about penises. This explains the problem of the orgasm gap to a large degree, and why the people who have fewest orgasms in their sexual relationships are cishet women.

According to various studies in 2011, 2013 and 2014, in which cis men and women identifying as heterosexual, homosexual or bisexual were interviewed, the heterosexual women had at least one orgasm 61.6 per cent of the times they had sex, while the lesbians did in 74.7 per cent of instances. The heterosexual men took first place with 85.5 per cent, and the homosexual men were a shade below on 84.7 per cent. Bisexual people declared rates of orgasm that were lower than that of the monosexuals (58 per cent for women and 77.6 per cent for men).

This gap is explained by the normalization of sexual practices that don't take into account the actual bodies of the majority of women, although it's curious that heterosexual men have more orgasms than gays. The summary isn't very flattering to cis men: if you want to have the best chance of having orgasms, choose someone from any other group as a sexual partner. Or at least try not to go to bed with a sexually illiterate man.

Another interesting bit of data is how long a sexual encounter lasts: it takes heterosexual couples between 15 and 30 minutes, while for lesbians it's between 30 and 60 minutes on average, depending on which study you look at. That is, cis lesbians have fewer orgasms than cis men, but they enjoy themselves for longer.

This is linked to the fact that, when there is a penis in the mix, there is no expectation of pleasure without an erection. Everything that occurs before coitus is considered 'foreplay', and once coitus is finished there's nothing else to be done. When coitus isn't considered essential, as in the case between people who don't have a penis, a thousand ways of finding pleasure open up for everyone participating.

In cishet encounters, the man's orgasm is at once the objective and the signal of the end of a sexual encounter. The woman's orgasm is secondary, and, if it doesn't come before the man's, completely expendable. Too many cis men take for granted that the party is over without bearing in mind whether their sexual partner is satisfied with what has gone on up to that point. This isn't a problem if it happens promptly – sometimes you just don't feel like drawing it out and you have the right to stop at any time you want to. Then again, if your sexual encounters are systematically centred on the selfish pursuit of pleasure which disregards the desires of the people you're having sex with, the problem is obvious.

A survey carried out by Sida Studi, of 500 young people between the ages of 14 and 16, shows that when sexual relations don't include intercourse, 44 per cent of girls state that they feel satisfied but, in contrast, only 22 per cent of boys are satisfied. The figures change dramatically when sexual relations include intercourse, in which case the boys are the ones most satisfied. This has a lot to do not only with the difference between practices that give pleasure to boys and those that give pleasure to girls, but, above all, with the expectations we have about what a satisfactory sexual relationship is. Women learn to expect less pleasure and content themselves with aspects of sexuality that don't focus on orgasmic pleasure (such as intimacy, trust, proximity) and this, added to the purely physical elements we've already mentioned, makes coitus have little bearing on their sexual satisfaction.

Since coitus is believed to be the core of sex, once a cis man has had an orgasm and the erection subsides, some consider the sexual encounter already over. Destroying this belief might not only increase pleasure for cis men's sexual partners, who perhaps don't need or want to stop when there is no possibility of coitus, it could also open up possibilities for cis men: they might discover that their bodies have a frontier of pleasures beyond what coitocentric culture has made us believe.

Losing virginity

According to the *Oxford English Dictionary* (*OED*), 'virgin' means 'a person that has no sexual experience'. But when someone is asked whether they're a virgin, the implication is that they're being asked whether they've had coitus or not, as if no other sexual activities really count. Many young people have sexual encounters but avoid intercourse for religious or social motives. The idea of virginity is desirable, especially for girls, and is associated with positive qualities related to femininity (modesty, chastity, sacrifice, lack of sexual desire), to the point that we have the expression 'losing virginity', as if it's a very valuable quality that you must keep while you're 'on the market'. Once you're coupled up (if not forever, at least for the foreseeable future), you can 'offer' your virginity to the lucky chosen one. In contrast, boys have to get rid of their virginity as soon as they can. This creates opposing tensions between heterosexual young people: while cis boys are under pressure to have intercourse as early as possible, cis girls are under pressure to have it for the first time with someone with whom they have a stable two-person relationship.

But, if losing virginity means maintaining sexual relationships, and we're not satisfied by the idea of them necessarily revolving around sexual intercourse, maybe we should establish more clearly what 'maintaining sexual relationships' means. For me, it means any physical contact that is born of shared desire and also seeks shared pleasure. Desire being shared is important – otherwise, we would enter into the terrain of rape, which plays no part in sexuality, but in the abuse of power instead.

If a sexual encounter is physical contact born of shared desire that seeks shared pleasure, determining *when* virginity is lost is complicated. Two people brushing fingers together in a gesture you might think is casual were it not for the accompanying look of complicity and the blushing, for me, is sex. But then I find my own definition narrow, because don't messages exchanged between people sometimes miles apart, which have the power to trigger the most intense desire, count as sex? Yes, they do. So contact doesn't necessarily need to be physical, there just needs to be contact.

In the same way that it can be difficult to know at what point we've shared this kind of contact with someone for the first time, there is a part of virginity that is never lost, if we see it as the absence of certain sexual activities. I'm sure there are a thousand things I still haven't done with anyone, and maybe never will, as well as some I can't imagine and will discover. It seems beautiful to me to think that, so many years after having begun to share my desire, I can still be surprised by how my body interacts with another body, how we invent pleasures as we get to know each other, how things that – with another person or in another context – leave me cold suddenly ignite an unknown pleasure within me.

To an extent, we're never virgins in every way, but always in some way.

All the pleasure in the world
And so, little by little, we've come to sexuality aside from coitus, which, for a change, has served in this chapter as foreplay, before reaching what I consider the important part. If we actually find limited, disappointing pleasure where we've been taught pleasure resides, it's time to take a risk and explore uncharted territory.

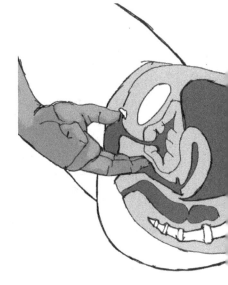

This is where we people with nonconforming sexual orientations and gender identities have had a head start: as a result of not being represented in the tame sex shown on TV, we've been led to improvise. For once, leaving norms behind works for us: the very fact of not being able to fulfil them forces us to act more freely. We're forced to inhabit bodies that seek one another, interrogate one another, listen to one another, explore one another. How lovely if everyone were to get there, to that state of freedom.

It's not entirely true that we nonconformists aren't steered towards anything in particular: there are a couple of supposed must-dos (anal penetration for cis gays, the famous scissoring for cis lesbians). But the simple fact of facing a body that resembles yours helps you know intuitively that there is pleasure beyond these. If you like to be touched *here*, or like *this* to be done to you, maybe the other person will too. On the other hand, the act of rejecting a norm as rigid as obligatory heterosexuality right from the start can help you reject others. When you feel deep inside that something that has been sold to you as the one and only absolute truth is a lie, it's easier for you to dare to question other assumed truths.

Obviously, being cishet doesn't stop you from exploring your sexuality. Luckily, many people find a way to go off-script. Unfortunately, this usually happens when you haven't been completely happy with your sex life for a while, and when you're more experienced and comfortable in your body and those of others. Better sex education should help de-mystify coitus on one hand, and make it clear that there isn't only one route to pleasure, on the other.

While the majority of bodies have so-called *erogenous* zones, which are more sensitive to pleasure because of the higher concentration of nerve endings there, a very important part of pleasure is about the construction of desire. When you've been thinking about someone for hours, feeling their hand on your shoulder can cause a burst of indescribable pleasure, while in another context your clitoris could be directly stimulated without you feeling much.

On one hand, we often uncritically expect certain parts of our bodies to automatically produce pleasure, but at the same time practices that could be very pleasurable stay hidden from us. This occurs as much because of social taboo as because of ignorance or lack of interest in how bodies function beyond the specific act of intercourse. We're not only conditioned by what we're supposed to like, but also by ideas about what we shouldn't like and by a lack of imagination about what we might like, because we don't know that these parts of our bodies can be used for pleasure.

For example, we know that stimulation of the prostate through anal penetration usually causes intense pleasure, but many cishet men consider the idea of being penetrated anally (with a penis, fingers or toys) unthinkable, because it would bring their masculinity into question. If you have a vulva, you also enjoy prostate stimulation through certain forms of vaginal penetration. This stimulation can cause ejaculation of a more watery, colourless and abundant fluid than normal. Ejaculation doesn't necessarily have to be linked to orgasm, and, depending on countless variables, it can be spectacular or very discreet. This is unfamiliar to the point that some cis women believe that they pee themselves during sexual relations, leading sometimes to discomfort and embarrassment. In fact, the existence of the female prostate wasn't acknowledged until quite recently and even now you'll rarely see it listed as a female attribute.

Wanna deflate expectations?

Preconceived ideas about what it means to be a man and what it means to be a woman are some of the greatest obstacles to everyone's pleasure. The stereotype of the man always poised at the ready, with an erection like a flag of desire, puts the sexuality of cis men under enormous pressure. The expectation of an erect penis completely conditions the sexuality of everyone who comes into contact with bodies with a penis, be they cis men or not.

If you're with a person with a penis that isn't erect, the first thing that crosses your mind might be that they don't desire you. But the connection between sexual desire and an erection isn't automatic and may be affected by many variables, ranging from the psychological (the pressure to become hard is itself inhibiting) to the physical (maybe the consumption of certain drugs or medications). Furthermore, there are people with a penis who can reach orgasm and ejaculation with practically no erection, and it's very common for there to be desire without an erection (at least initially). On the other hand, expecting a penis to remain permanently erect for a session of sex lasting a good while (and good sex usually takes time) is unrealistic.

Eliminating coitus from the core of sexuality is the best way of exploring possibilities for pleasure that don't involve an erection, or even a penis. But for that, it's necessary for all the people involved in the sexual encounter, starting with the owner of the penis, to be willing. This is more complicated than it seems when all your life you've been made to believe that fucking is putting a dick in a hole, preferably a vagina.

On the other hand, women are expected to be passive objects that don't feel desire, or, if they do, not to show it. Even though, on a rational level, they might think that they've overcome it and are mistresses of their sexuality, this interiorized belief can make it difficult for them to express their sexual preferences, especially if they contradict supposedly 'normal' practices. In general, women find it easier to say 'Put it inside me', than to say 'Put two fingers inside me gently, then apply some stronger pressure while you go down on me', however much more potential for orgasmic success this second way of putting things might have. Likewise, non-verbal directions like guiding a hand or mouth to a body part with a gesture, can also be difficult.

Communication (whether verbal or not) is the foundation of shared pleasure and the essential construction of consent. We'll talk about this in more detail in the next chapter, but it's important to keep in mind that explaining what we like is the first step towards more satisfying sex.

Come, come!

In general, enjoying yourself isn't a foregone conclusion. You can force someone to do something, but not to enjoy themselves while they do it. In contrast, as we've seen, it seems that the aim of sex is to have an orgasm (or at least for the cis man to have one). So sex in which the cis man doesn't orgasm is considered 'failure'. Once again, preconceived ideas limit possibilities for pleasure.

The pressure to orgasm isn't exclusive to cis men, however. In fact, despite the orgasm gap and the generally sketchy knowledge about bodies with a vulva, the heterosexual couple's simultaneous orgasm myth is fairly widespread. 'Frigid' or 'dried-up cunt' are regular insults for women, often even used together, as if the woman is to blame for not feeling sexual pleasure as well as for the sexual ineptitude of their partners. If we recall the statistic from a few pages ago, cishet women don't orgasm in close to 40 per cent of their sexual encounters. This in no way means that they don't feel pleasure. In a hyper-sexualized society such as ours, in which having orgasms is deemed a sign of success, there are a significant number of women who believe that they should be having orgasms when they just aren't, and the false beliefs about sexuality we grow up with don't help women to understand why they aren't happening, and even less to remove the pressure to have one.

A myth about the wonder dick has arisen, a kind of magic wand that alone satisfies the sexual needs of all the people involved in an encounter. The cis man can fall back on the expectation of an erection, the obligation to orgasm and even the responsibility of causing coitus so fantastic it makes the cis woman come without having to do anything else.

For fear of disappointing their sexual partner's expectations, many women pretend that they have orgasms in these situations, and thus reinforce the idea that orgasms through penetrative sex happen more often than they actually do. Cishet women who admit to having faked orgasms at some point in their lives (that is, almost all) have given various reasons when surveyed. The most usual ones are to avoid making their partner feel bad, or because they're not enjoying the sexual encounter and want it to end as soon as possible (and they don't think simply saying 'Stop' is a possibility). The latter is especially worrying.

Pretending can be a valid strategy in a sporadic hook-up when you don't feel like giving explanations and you don't feel strong enough to say when enough is enough. Within a couple, however, systematically faking suggests that you aren't enjoying specific acts, or the conditions surrounding them, and it can perpetuate dissatisfaction and open the door to resentment. If he isn't particularly bothered about knowing whether she's really having a good time and she fakes orgasms so he leaves her in peace, they may have an important conversation looming.

Along with the notion of an orgasm being obligatory is the idea that if you have one – and only one – the job's done. That is, assuming you're lucky enough to have sexual encounters where there's been frank discussion about closing the orgasm gap, sex only ends when everyone has had an orgasm. This is clearly a step forward from the notion that sex ends when the

Fuck, sleep with, make love, dance the naked dance, do it, lay, roger, bang, screw, make the beast with two backs, shaft, poke, ride, shag, hump, get it on, fornicate, copulate, do the business, bonk, mate, roll in the hay, possess, knock off, have it off, smash, pound, hump, go all the way.

cishet man comes, but it doesn't take into account that many people who have a vulva (and some who have a penis) can have several orgasms in a relatively short space of time, and that it's perfectly possible to enjoy 'sessions' 3 or 4 hours long when you are all having orgasms. Ideally, a sexual encounter should end (unless someone wants to stop beforehand, for whatever reason) when the people participating feel satiated and satisfied, whether they've had 25 orgasms or none.

If we eliminate the orgasm as the final objective of sexual encounters and accept it as just another possibility, we may discover an interest in pleasurable sensations that we'd never have tried if we were looking for shortcuts. In short, pleasure is a right, not an obligation.

Why fuck?

'Why', the fundamental question that pushes humanity forward, is one of the questions we ask ourselves the least when it comes to sex. Maybe the answer is obvious: we have sex with the aim of sharing sexual pleasure. But sex is a form of human interaction that goes much further than this and is influenced by the power relations present in societies.

There are very strict rules about what is considered 'normal' when it comes to sexual encounters, who can enjoy them and how, and one of the goals of this book is to reflect on all these rules and how to free ourselves of them if we so choose. At the same time, not having a sexual life if you're an adult in our society is considered abnormal and undesirable.

Many people have sexual encounters when they reach adolescence because it's expected, not thinking any more about it, and sometimes agreeing to acts that aren't particularly satisfying simply 'because that's what's done' or what they think 'is done'. You can fuck out of curiosity, to feel more grown-up, to try new things or even out of boredom.

You can also fuck to please your partner. This isn't negative per se; we can decide to accept or even initiate a sexual encounter at a time that we don't particularly feel like it (but it doesn't bother us, either) because we know that the other person does and there's no harm in trying it and seeing whether we get into it. But there's a problem when having sex is considered an obligation which we have to go through every so often, whether we want to or not.

Within traditional religious frameworks, the husband's sexual satisfaction was historically considered the wife's obligation, to the point that marital rape was legal across the West until relatively recently. Even though this idea is no longer explicitly worded this way, there is certainly a belief that in a stable heterosexual couple the woman should 'give in' to the man's desire if he feels like having sex. This is one of the many pillars of what is called *rape culture*, which we will analyse in the next chapter.

Another reason some people have sex is because they like showing and receiving affection. If this is the case, we could consider caresses, kisses and – not necessarily sexual – physical proximity, which will reinforce the bond between the people involved without any of the pressure that can be felt during sex.

Analysing why we have the sex we have and who we have it with can help us to detect abusive or exploitative situations, to feel freer to say no and to initiate sex when we want to. On the other hand, if we get used to listening to the voice of our own desire, we can also learn to tune in to the desire of others. This will result in a sexual life that is more pleasurable and better suited to our needs, free from the absurd obligations and rules that encumber us.

What porn doesn't show

According to a worldwide survey of 19,000 people by BitDefender, 95 per cent of adults with dependent minors who have a computer know that the children watch porn on it (because they've found out from the browser history). The average age they start to watch porn is eleven (meaning that there are many younger than eleven who watch it) and the distribution of consumption by gender is significant: 90 per cent of boys and 60 per cent of girls access porn. When it comes to the adult population, PornHub, one of the most-visited portals, states that its clientele consists of 76 per cent men and 24 per cent women.

Increasingly more and increasingly younger people are watching commercial porn. Undeniably, what it shows us affects our attitudes towards sex. It conditions what expectations we have and which practices we normalize and consider desirable, but we are also enormously conditioned by what we don't see. As well as reinforcing a coitocentric sexuality based on the pleasure of cis men, it conceals an infinite number of practices. It invests sexuality with mechanical seriousness and gymnastic exercise and strips it of tenderness and of happiness: in short, of humanity. As occurs in the case of any medium transmitting stereotypes, the problem with most commercial pornography isn't that what it shows isn't possible or is a 'lie'. The problem is that it's not the *only* possible sexuality, or even the most desirable. And as with any cultural representation, that's all it is – a *representation*. Young people who take it as a kind of *school* of sexuality, who believe that imitating it is a good way to 'fuck well', will certainly be disappointed and miss out on a whole array of intriguing feelings.

Among the things that don't usually emerge in *mainstream* porn is the rapport born of laughter. Sex can lead to many potentially comic moments, from the typical accidental bang of the head against the wall, to the difficulty of taking off tight trousers or unwieldy bras. We find it normal to laugh or smile when we're having a good time in almost all contexts, but it seems to be forbidden during sex. It's as if giving space to laughter might break some kind of magic. Personally, what really seems magic to me is sharing so much mutual trust with someone that I could crack up mid-fuck then calmly go on with what we were doing. On the other hand, there are people who have fits of laughter (or crying) after an orgasm. It's important to give space so that no one feels ashamed.

We don't usually see porn actors having their period either. Many people state that their sexual desire increases during menstruation. Even though fucking when you have your period has been a taboo for a long time, and there are people who prefer not to do it unless it's with someone they trust deeply, others do it all the time. Certain activities, such as oral sex or penetration, aren't recommended while you have your period because the risk of catching sexually transmitted infections is higher, but outside of that there is no reason not to. If you're concerned about dirtying the sheets, just put a dark towel over them.

We don't see *valuable* communication in porn either. Sometimes things are said, but generally when 'Do you like that?' is asked, there is no kind of space to respond with 'No'. The script always says 'Yes, yes, more', even though it might be more realistic to say 'Erm . . . not really'. The belief that we'll know what our partner wants through mere intuition, or that they will know what we want, is absurd.

If sex lasts longer than the regulation 20 minutes that marks the average within heterosexual relationships, it's possible that at some point you'll be thirsty, hungry or need to go to the toilet. Many people with a vulva need to pee after having an orgasm (it may be linked to squirting if this fluid doesn't come out when the prostate is stimulated), and besides it's recommended for preventing urine infections. Urine is used in porn for sexual games, but saying 'Wait a second, I'm going to the toilet' isn't in the script. Yet in real life this often happens.

Because these things happen, the situation requires time, trust and comfort. These values aren't exactly embraced by *mainstream* pornography, yet, in contrast, they contribute enormously to the satisfaction of everyone taking part.

Choose your own adventure

Apart from vaginal and anal penetration (with fingers, penis or toys) and oral sex (stimulating the vulva, penis, testicles or anus with the mouth), which are the practices most often seen in pornography and the most well-known in general, there are virtually infinite combinations that can give us pleasure. Any part of the body that we can caress, kiss, rub, lick, blow on, or apply cold or heat, pressure, etc., to is capable of producing pleasure.

You may have noticed that in many cases in this chapter (and the rest of the book) I speak as if there are by default two people in sexual encounters. It's the most common combination, but it's certainly not the only one. When you embark on the adventure of a shared journey, sexual pleasure and arousal tend to be reciprocal and are nourished between the people involved. You only have to open yourself up to listening and allowing yourself to speak, with your tongue and with your body.

~~consent~~ enthusiasm

Sharing desire, sharing pleasure – as nice as it sounds and just as easy, if you're clear on a few things. This is what makes it complicated: we're surrounded by a world contriving to stop us from seeing clearly. Remembering that *healthy* sexual relationships are contact born of shared desire and seeking similarly shared pleasure can help us when we're unsure.

Consent is the minimum needed for sexual encounters to be sexual encounters (whether healthy or not so healthy), and not *rape*. When you have sexual contact with someone who doesn't consent to it, this is forced sexual contact, and therefore crosses the line of what is legal. It could technically be called abuse, harassment or rape, depending on the circumstances. This affects how harsh a prison sentence might be, but in any case it's no longer sex: specifically, it's a crime against *sexual freedom*.

We come across common sayings that sum up the general agreement about what it is to consent, such as 'When no one says anything, everyone agrees', or 'Anyone who doesn't speak consents.' Behind this point of view lies the notion that we can take for granted that consent exists until we're told otherwise, and a large part of the population agrees with this. But, clearly, it's not that simple. Someone not saying they don't consent isn't enough for us to be able to say we can assume they do:

certain socially accepted conditions are required. For example, we can assume that we don't have consent to touch a person we don't know, whom we've never spoken to and whom we meet on the street, despite the fact that they haven't explicitly said 'Don't touch me.'

When consent is discussed in public, some call for it to be explicit. That is, to be sure that a sexual encounter is consensual and therefore not rape, everyone involved should explicitly say that they are on the same page. Those who want to carry this argument to absurd lengths have it easy – all of us with a sex life have had sexual encounters (often, *healthy* sexual encounters) in which no one has said anything yet everyone has been very happy to participate.

Then again, why are there people who are so disturbed by the idea of explicitly requesting and showing that yes, we do like it, we do want it? This can be explained by certain beliefs shared by a significant proportion of the population and sustained by what is called *rape culture*. That is, there are attitudes and beliefs about sexualities and gender which lead to a large part of non-consensual sexual encounters (that is, *rapes*) being considered normal, acceptable or even desirable. In a society where everyone is in theory opposed to rape, rape culture drives the normalization and acceptance of sexual violence (that is, rape). This is done by sidestepping the definition of *rape* (according to the *OED*, 'the act of forced, non-consenting, or illegal sexual intercourse with another person') and creating the stereotype in which this 'carnal act' is perpetrated by a male stranger, possibly a migrant or madman, in a dark doorway, using physical violence.

The reality, shown by statistics produced by the police, informs us that in the majority of cases the rapists are indeed men, but they are not strangers. They are the victims' partners, their friends, their relatives. Men the victims trust and who seem to love them. But if these men love women, why do they rape them? Because they're convinced that what they're doing isn't rape, but something else. It's forcing a little, insisting until kingdom come, exercising conjugal rights. Many rapists don't realize that they're doing anything wrong, or don't consider 'forcing' to be 'raping', or believe that 'forcing' is justified in certain circumstances.

A study done at a US university indicates that 31.7 per cent of men surveyed would rape if they knew there would be no consequences of any kind. How can it be that a third of men can state something as enormously outrageous as this? The trick is in how the question is phrased. The question was: 'Would you have sexual relations with a woman against her will, if you were sure no one would know and there wouldn't be consequences?' When later asked 'Would you rape a woman, if you were sure no one would know and there wouldn't be consequences?', 13.6 per cent (which is still a very high figure) continued to respond in the affirmative. This last group were openly hostile towards women and explicitly considered them to be inferior to men. The others didn't state it so baldly, nor were they aware that 'having sexual intercourse against someone's will' is 'raping'.

This is why it is so important to call things by their name and unmask the ideological pillars sustaining rape culture. Fighting these attitudes and these beliefs in others – but also in ourselves when we have internalized them – should help us to enjoy a freer, happier and more respectful sexuality.

Men don't know how to control themselves

Myth tells us that women have a lower libido than men, and because of that they don't understand that men can't control themselves when they're turned on. Such a gross (and ill-founded) generalization suggests that men are animals that can't control their instincts, and therefore raping is acceptable.

As we've seen, this 'raping' is more indirectly expressed as 'forcing' or 'not taking women's desires into account'.

Even though the majority of people who rape are men, the majority of men are not rapists. If they truly couldn't contain themselves, or it had something to do with testosterone (as many people state) and was a biological fact, we'd have to expect the majority of men to be rapists. Even as discouraging a study as the one we've just mentioned concludes that almost 70 per cent of men would not rape, even if no one were to know and there would be no consequences. This alone dismantles the idea that raping is an unstoppable instinct.

Besides, rapists know perfectly well how to restrain themselves: they choose the right moment so they don't get caught, victims who are least likely to report them and a way to manipulate the facts so that, if they are reported, they can cast doubt on whether there was consent or not. If it were a matter of nature, rapes would be occurring at any time, anywhere, to anyone, with no consideration of the most favourable circumstances for not getting caught. Men know how to control themselves as well as anyone else. What happens is that some don't want to control themselves and, given the few consequences there usually are for committing rape, the system contributes to there being no incentive for doing so beyond their own conscience.

She actually wanted to

It isn't completely clear whether this phrase, which is heard more often than is understandable in the twenty-first century when discussing a rape, is an excuse rapists use for justification when they get caught (they didn't realize they were committing rape because they thought there was consent) or whether they really can't distinguish between a relationship that is consensual and one that isn't. If you were wearing sexy clothes, maybe you wanted to. If you'd been drinking, maybe you don't remember that you wanted to. If you lead a promiscuous life, you surely wanted to this time too. If you became petrified and you didn't say no, or if you said no but didn't violently fight the rapist off, it was impossible for him to know you didn't want to.

Lack of interest in sexuality is one of the values associated with femininity; women agreeing to sexual relations (with men, obviously) out of love – and only out of love, not because they want to – is considered positive. Again, it's not generally framed as overtly, but in the education of girls and the disciplining of women there is something known as *slut shaming*, which consists of trying to shame women who demonstrate their sexuality: don't dress like that, you look like a tart; don't show you like him, he'll lose respect for you; don't drop hints, he'll take you for a slut. By persuading women not to show their desire, we leave them without any weapon to demonstrate their lack of consent: if you're persuaded that when you mean 'yes', you must say 'no', how do you say 'no' when you mean 'no'. The feminist slogan 'No means no' is a step towards breaking this vicious circle, and one more is the blunt 'Only yes means yes', which seeks explicit consent, constructed while the sexual encounter lasts and renewed as often as necessary.

On the other hand, for someone who doesn't mind satisfying themselves sexually regardless of whether the other person likes it or not, it's very comfortable to lean on the 'philosophy' of conquest. Most of the time, 'I didn't know that this person didn't want to' really means 'I didn't want to know that this person didn't want to' or, even worse, 'I didn't care at all whether this person wanted to or not.'

Finally, there is a belief that if a vulva is wet or a penis is erect, that person wants sex. This isn't as automatic as it seems. Certain physical stimuli can trigger physical reactions (such as lubrication or erection), regardless of whether the person feels comfortable in the situation or not. There have even been cases of people who have had orgasms during rape. This doesn't mean 'they wanted it'. A specific physical reaction doesn't necessarily mean consent.

The 'dead' woman

The ads and photographs of models we see often show, on the one hand, an active man, winning women as if they are trophies, and on the other, motionless women, ever thinner, ever paler, ever more dead. A specific type of advertising wants to present the dead – or seemingly so – woman as ultimately desirable. Mainstream pornography also contributes to the stereotype of the passive woman in sexual encounters, who does what she is told to do or accepts what is done to her, without will or desire.

We grow up normalizing one-way sexual encounters, from an active subject (the man) that fucks a passive object (usually a woman), instead of two-way, communicative encounters in which you fuck with, not *against*, someone. We assume that men must take the initiative and women must let them, to such an extent that there are men who feel violent when their sexual partners ask for specific sexual practices, and women who aren't capable of saying 'I don't like it like that, let's try it this way', when they're not having a good time in bed (or wherever).

We've seen recent judicial sentences such as in the 'Wolf Pack' case, in which judges who had seen a video of a motionless woman, showing no initiative at all, surrounded by five men treating her as if she were an inflatable doll, stated that it wasn't clear that there was no consent and she 'looked like she was having a good time'. This so-called 'good time', was five men, including a policeman and a soldier, who referred to themselves as the 'Wolf Pack', gang-raping an eighteen-year-old woman and filming themselves repeatedly attacking her in Pamplona in July 2016. When they were brought to trial in 2018, the men were found guilty of abuse but not rape, as the judges saw no signs of violence or intimidation being used against the girl, and suggested that what occurred were 'sexual acts in an atmosphere of revelry and delight'. This verdict led to outrage and widespread protests throughout Spain, and eventually their convictions were upgraded to sexual assault. You really have to have internalized the belief that women are objects to believe something like that, whether you're one of the five rapists or a complicit judge.

Sexual relations as a right

Of course, everyone has a right to their sexuality and to explore what they desire. This in no way means that there is any kind of right to have sexual relations with other people. However frustrating it might be to want to go to bed with someone and for it not to happen, this doesn't in any way justify rape. Not only is masturbation an excellent source of self-exploration and a healthy, recommended sexual practice, it can also help us to bear frustration better.

There is a group of execrable men who call themselves INCELs (from 'involuntary celibate') who claim that the fact that women don't want to have sex with them infringes their rights. Keeping in mind that they are a group of avowed misogynists and racists, what I'd find strange is them being able to find people who wanted to sleep with them at all. Expecting a woman to 'do you a favour', believing you have a right to it, is the ultimate expression of rape culture.

While not reaching the ultimate stupidity of INCEL premises, there is indeed a general notion that men deserve to have sex and *it's no big deal for women* to give in. One of the most absurd arguments used to try and persuade me to fuck was 'Come on, it'll only be five minutes.' I didn't feel like it precisely because I knew it would only be five minutes, and what I wanted or whether I'd like it to last longer wouldn't even cross that person's mind.

The concept of sexual autonomy is much more interesting. As a person with a particular sexuality, I decide for myself which paths I want to explore, and take charge of my desire and my pleasure. This autonomy plays with the autonomies of others, and of course we can freely decide to come together. In the search for pleasure, every person must take responsibility for their own experience and, at the same time, ensure that they respect the experience of the other people sharing the adventure. Without owing anything to anyone, we can opt for generosity. Without anyone owing us anything, we can ask for what we'd like.

Beyond men and women

Clearly, the gender mandate is a determining factor in rape culture, but it goes beyond the two groups commonly accepted as the only ones: cis men and cis women. Rape culture actually strengthens the macho figure, which is a specific type of man that has the permission and mandate to dominate not only women, but any person that isn't a 'real' man.

The construction of toxic masculinity rewards men who behave in a dominant, violent and predatory manner, and places the rest of humanity into a group of controllable – and, if it comes to it – rapable people. Apart from the diehard believers, the system relies on those who don't want to be rapable and therefore adopt the macho role, even if only in appearance.

Within the groups of men who shout things at unknown women in the street, there are only one or two who shout, and many who stay quiet. Taking issue with the behaviour of machos means leaving their group and therefore being in danger. You need to be very brave to do so, or your position has to have become truly unbearable.

Constructing enthusiastic consent

Up to now, we've seen how rape culture helps justify those who dispense with consent – that is, those who rape. But, without wading into the field of crime, the idea that to have sexual relations with someone all you need is for them to give consent chills my blood. 'To consent', according to the *OED*, is to 'voluntarily agree to a proposal, request, demand etc.; acquiesce'. When it's only about *consent*, ideas of both desire and pleasure disappear. We should ask ourselves if we want sex with someone who isn't doing it out of desire, out of pleasure – who agrees, who acquiesces. My answer is *no*. I want enthusiastic sexual encounters with people who are dying to do it. With people who desire me – who spend a long time thinking about what they want to do, explore, invent together. Alternatively, I can do it all alone: I know myself and love myself and can have a great time without needing to bother anyone.

'Consenting' may be about social pressure, the other person insisting, insecurity . . . Enthusiasm is unmistakable: it's about desire. If you resign yourself to 'consent', you're missing out on an essential part of sharing, as well as putting someone in an unpleasant situation.

It might seem that, living in such a potent rape culture, we can't do anything but accept consensual relationships, even though there's no enthusiasm. After all, if they are consensual, at least no one is being raped. But this is not true: despite everything seeming to point to the contrary, many people prefer healthy sexual relationships. Let's remind ourselves what they are: relationships that are born of shared desire and seek shared pleasure.

So, for a start, we need to be sure of two things: that the other person desires us, and that we desire the other person. For all the reasons we've previously discussed, the first part is especially important if you have been educated to be a man; the second part is especially important if you have been educated to be a woman; neither is expendable. Once we've established that this is the case, a journey begins. It may be long or short, but it requires communication for it to be pleasant for everyone. The communication needn't necessarily be verbal in all cases, but it must exist.

Even though we can be generally aroused by whatever is proposed by someone we're very attracted to, it's likely there are things that annoy us, that we don't feel like at the time, or that we just find so-so. Telepathy doesn't exist: we can't read our sexual partners' minds, nor can they read ours.

When you know someone very well, you may be able to read their body language and adequately decipher messages that go unnoticed by other people. This isn't telepathy, it's communication. Communication isn't always verbal, nor must consent be, but the less we know the other person, the more important it is to clarify verbally that there are no misunderstandings.

When we talk about 'constructing consent', it must be kept in mind that consent isn't permission given once (by action or omission) and sufficient forever more. It's an agreement that can change every time circumstances change. There is a very famous video (which you can find on social networks if you search *consent as a cup of tea*) that explains consent as if it were drinking a cup of tea. Perhaps you think you feel like one and then it turns out that you don't, or you fall asleep, or you don't like that tea. Perhaps one day you felt like tea and drank it, and another day you don't want it. The fact that it seems like a good idea to have sex with someone at one time doesn't imply an obligation to continue if something is making you uncomfortable, nor does it give the other person the right to force you or make you feel bad for refusing.

People deserve the respect they offer: someone friendly, who offers something without pressing or insisting, deserves a friendly response, which can be 'no, thank you', or 'I like you very much, but I don't want to right now.' Someone who doesn't keep you in mind and wants to put pressure on you, through emotional blackmail or other strategies, deserves a firm response, and if they cross the line of violence, you have the right to defend yourself with any tools you need.

What is NOT consent

There are circumstances in which not saying 'no' or even saying 'yes' doesn't necessarily mean there is consent. Every time we want to have sex with someone, we have the responsibility of ensuring that this person does so freely and feels that they can refuse or stop at any time without there being negative consequences (and, obviously, that we can too).

What if the person is drunk or high? Maybe you really want to be with this person, and it may even be that at some point before getting intoxicated this person has let you know they really want to be with you too. But if, later, they are clearly drunk or high, it's better to leave it for another day. The world won't end if you don't fuck today: tomorrow, next week or another time when everyone is sober, you'll certainly have a better time and there'll also be no doubt that everyone is doing what they want to.

If there is a power imbalance between the two that could make the person in a subordinate position feel unable to say no, it's necessary to bear that in mind and determine whether it's worth the risk of inappropriately putting pressure on someone. Teacher/student, boss/worker, relationships in which there is a significant difference in age/power/money, relationships in which one of the people belongs to a group oppressed by racism, transphobia ... When we're in a position of power, perhaps the most respectful thing is to hope that the other person will be the one to take the initiative. That way, it's easier to be sure we aren't putting pressure on them.

If one of the people consents because the other has lied about things that matter to them, from a legal viewpoint it is considered that there is no consent. For example, if using a condom has been agreed and at some point the person wearing it takes it off without saying so, this is rape and sentences have been imposed for this reason. Another typical instance is when one of the people lies about having other partners – there are many people for whom it is important not to be with anyone who has other relationships and who wouldn't consent if they knew what was going on.

The sexiest word is yes

Some say that making consent explicit kills the game of seduction. In this Hollywood romanticizing of relationships, the idea is that when there is a lot of chemistry between two people, a kind of telepathy is established which makes them know exactly what the other person wants. As is obvious, this gives rise to all kinds of misunderstandings, because it's already been made clear that telepathy doesn't exist and there is nothing easier than misinterpreting someone you don't know.

Traditional seduction is based on a hunter and prey; the hunter besieges the prey until it falls. In this cliché of romantic comedies, the (obviously male) hunter-predator stops at nothing to catch his (obviously female) prey. The idea that insistence will lead to victory is highly damaging, because many of these scavengers don't let it go with the first 'no', when maybe the prey wants to do her own thing or be with other people. And it's doubly perverse because of its flip side: 'If you don't insist, she'll think you don't care.'

> **consent**
>
> [12th century; from French *consent*]
>
> *1* Voluntary agreement to a proposal, request, demand etc.; acquiescence. Permission or approval for something.
>
> *2* Voluntary agreement to sexual intercourse or other sexual activity by a person who has the (legal) freedom and capacity to make such a choice.
>
> See also **age of consent** n., **non-consent** n.

From my point of view, spoken communication and respect for the limits placed on us don't destroy seduction, but rather turn it into a game of intrigue in which anyone participating is doing so with desire – and not fear – as the driver: a seduction spurred on by the other party's desire, in which it's inconceivable to force anything unreciprocated. A seduction to be played, to be experienced, to be enjoyed. In short, a seduction that leads to not only consensual, but enthusiastic, sexual encounters.

I thoroughly recommend the recently released book *La paraula més sexi és sí* [The Sexiest Word Is Yes] by the writer Shaina Joy Machlus (translated by Núria Parés, and published by L'Altra) not long ago, in which she speaks extensively about consent and how to transform rape culture into respect culture. We can shatter the idea that talking isn't sexy, for a start.

Consent in stable relationships

It may seem that in a stable relationship, consent goes without saying. Even though in general we usually feel more free to seek physical proximity and make sexual insinuations to someone we maintain a stable relationship with, we mustn't take for granted that every time one person feels like sex, the other has to agree to it.

On the other hand, there are couples who find some practices they like, get used to them and then find it hard to innovate. Talking about what gets us excited, what arouses our curiosity, what we want to try and what makes us uncomfortable can be a way of spurring on desire and getting out of the rut (if you don't like the rut). If we compare it to clothes, it would be like seeking accessories that we don't usually wear and that refresh and renew the clothes we know we're comfortable in.

A big part of sexual pleasure comes from thinking about it, imagining it, wanting it. If we let our partner know that in the future we'd like to try a specific sexual practice we haven't tried before, we give them time to consider whether they're turned on by it or not, whether it's something they feel comfortable with, and also to make 'counter offers' in case they decide against it. It's a way of drawing out the sexual play, as well as giving us time to decide.

Many people feel embarrassed when making specific suggestions or requests, and feel awful if the other person seems shocked or uncomfortable. If we establish a climate of communication in which we give each other permission to ask for what we like, while simultaneously leaving space for the other person to refuse, we'll have more freedom to explore new sensations. What's more, if we really know we can stop at any time, we'll also feel more comfortable experimenting. Faced with a new suggestion, maybe I won't know for sure whether I want to or not. It's marvellous to give space to doubt, to be able to try it and continue if it turns me on, and stop if I'm not into it. To know that I can say 'Okay, let's try it', and if I'm not sure, 'I'm not enjoying it, I prefer doing this', and return to the safe space of practices we love.

This kind of open and respectful communication promotes bonding with the other person and can be a great source of mutual pleasure. The questionnaire at the end of the book might be a way to bring it up – it's a list of different practices, and the idea is that each person individually marks which they would like to try, which they would never try, and which would be a maybe, but with reservations. Then you share the results and . . . fun times! The questionnaire is also infinitely expandable, and can include as many practices as we can come up with.

Warning signs

Rape culture is so present and so normalized that we don't recognize the reason for the discomfort we often feel regarding our sexuality or regarding our partner. There doesn't seem to be anything that stands out or anything *abnormal* in what we do or what happens to us, but we feel that something's not right. Especially if you've been educated to be a woman, or you belong to a group discriminated against for other reasons. Here are some warning signs.

– If sex is always initiated by the other person. Even though there are people who find it difficult to initiate sexual encounters because of education or shyness, if every time you have sex it is because someone else has suggested it, maybe it's time to consider whether you really feel like it or whether there are other reasons for agreeing.

– If you are always the passive one during sexual relations, letting it happen and never acting on your own initiative. Everyone experiences sexual relationships in a different way and doing any specific thing isn't obligatory, but extreme passivity can be a symptom of yielding to the desires of others without considering your own. You can also think about what things you would like to happen, what would turn you on more. Perhaps you don't even need to do it – imagining is also an active experience.

– If you don't feel pleasure during sexual encounters. Everyone has days when they are more inspired and they have fun during sex, and dull days when it's not all that great. But if, in general, you don't feel any kind of pleasure during sex, you probably have some sort of issue with the other person in your relationship. If you feel disgust or rejection: alarm bells. Even though your head is saying you've consented and it's no big deal, your body is telling you that something isn't right.

– If certain practices cause you discomfort or pain (and you don't like pain in sex). You can occasionally put up with a position or a practice that isn't the most comfortable in the world for a while, but if your partner repeatedly wants to do things that make you uncomfortable or hurt you, the most sensible thing is to say so. You can both certainly figure out a way for everyone to feel good.

– If you want it to end as soon as possible. It may be that you don't really feel like it – you've started thinking you'd get into it and in the end you realize you haven't but decide to plough on regardless. This happening once or twice is no tragedy, but if it often happens you must work out why. If there is no desire or pleasure, why are you having sex?

– If you need to disassociate from what is happening. Many people who have suffered sexual abuse in childhood or repeated rapes within the structure of a couple learn to disassociate during sex or specific practices. Disassociation can range from involuntary disconnection with the reality that you're living to forcing yourself to think about other things. This can reinforce post-traumatic stress and it's important to face it. If you don't want to discuss it with the person you have sex with, you can seek professional help, or help from your friends. Look for a support network that will listen and help you to recover.

– If you usually agree because you love the other person, but sex doesn't particularly interest you, or sex with this person doesn't particularly interest you. Socially, it's taken for granted that if you have a partner you have to have sex with them. Asexual people are one of the groups that experience more normalized sexual violence, because many other people don't understand that sex doesn't interest them. If you are asexual, you have every right to be loved and respected, and you will find people to establish healthy emotional relationships with who won't blackmail you by offering affection in exchange for sex.

– If, after sex, you feel emptiness, sadness, frustration or resentment towards the other person. Perhaps you're with someone who loves you very much, you want to have sex with them, but you usually feel terrible afterwards. Maybe deep down you feel this person doesn't suit you, they aren't really concerned with your pleasure, or you always end up putting their needs ahead of your own. Naming these feelings can be difficult, but trying might help you generally to be happier, and specifically to enjoy sex more.

To sum up, if you don't feel desire or pleasure, why are you having sex? Are you sure you want to continue?

enthusiasm

Of multiple origins. Partly a borrowing from Latin. Partly a borrowing from Greek.

[From post-classical Latin *enthusiasmus* 'inspiration, frenzy' (3rd cent); from the Gr. *enthousiasmós* 'ecstasy' 'being inspired or possessed by a god, alteration'.

m *1* RELIG Excessive religious emotion or fervour; mystical, fanatical or radical religious delusion. Now historical.

2 Strong emotion or fervour infusing poetry; impassioned poetical mood or tone. Obsolete.

3 Keen interest in, passion for, or enjoyment of a particular activity or subject; approval of or optimism about someone or something; eagerness, energy.

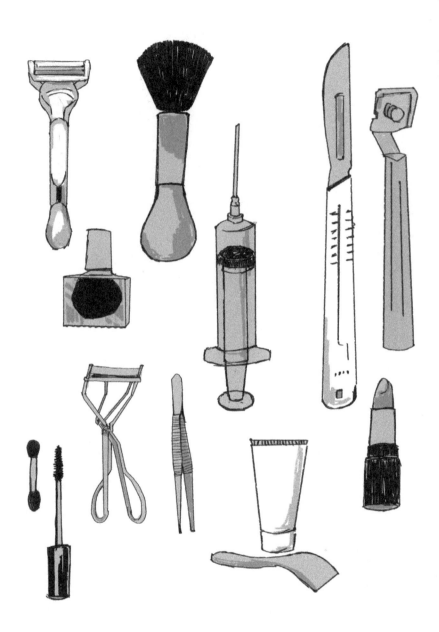

~~beauty~~
expectations

Sexual attraction is linked to the beauty of the person who attracts us, or so the idea goes. The more beautiful they are, the more attracted we are to them. This idea doesn't hold up at all, because physical attraction is composed of many factors, and we need only analyse which people we have been attracted to to see the variety.

Desirability – that is, the social consensus on which people are desirable and which are not – is another thing altogether. It's a question not merely of prized or reviled physical traits, but of other characteristics that can often be inferred from appearance, such as social class, too. We seem to find a person valued highly by society more attractive – or at least this makes it easier to explain publicly why we find them attractive.

Beauty brainwashing

It's easy to confuse what we should like with what we really like, especially because taste is acquired. Childhood is a training period in which society suggests not only what new members should be like when they grow up, but also what they shouldn't even go near. Everyone participates in the social control which makes the universe of possibility narrower and narrower by praising the little ones who have desirable looks and conduct and punishing those who don't. This training period has a practical aspect: not tolerating dangerous behaviour (gratuitously violent behaviour, for example) helps us to coexist. Then again, when the social rules established to protect us end up becoming an ever longer list of physical requirements that must be met to be 'acceptable', and that is an impossible list to boot, they carry more weight as the tools of oppression than of protection. We learn to reject the parts of ourselves that don't 'fit' long before being able to distinguish between what helps us and what harms us. We learn to hate our bodies when we should be learning to look after them, explore them, enjoy them. And while we're learning to hate our own bodies, we learn to reject non-normative bodies at the same time.

There are many examples demonstrating the utter arbitrariness of what we think is beautiful and what we think is disgusting. The same unshaven legs will cause indifference if we attribute them to a man and rejection if we attribute them to a woman, without any objective distinction to justify seeing them as more or less desirable. We've been educated to believe that women shouldn't have hair on their legs but men should, and therefore we think it desirable that women don't have any, yet it's all the same to us whether men do. This aesthetic criterion is being transformed by the increasing pressure on men to remove hair, as younger generations are beginning to find men without body hair desirable too. This pressure isn't harmless: hair removal costs money and there's a growing business of magic creams, supersonic devices and futuristic lasers promising to remove hair from wherever it's not supposed to be, and this wherever extends to more and more of the body. The cosmetic industry is reinforced by advertising, and advertising sustains the prevailing aesthetic standards at the same time as it nourishes them. It's a fish that bites its own tail, but far from devouring itself, it gets fatter and fatter. Such is the power of the pressure on appearance that we give in to it even when it goes against medical advice, as in the case of removing hair from genitals, wearing high heels, extreme weight control, and so on.

When we say a person is pretty, what we mean is that they fit the prevailing standards of beauty in our society at this time. Beauty standards vary in time and space, and this shows that there is no objective beauty, but only temporal and cultural preferences. Of course, there are some traits that we generally prefer or detest, but only very few.

Accept your body if it's beautiful

We learn what physical beauty means because we see certain body types presented as beautiful time and again, and we learn that physical beauty is important because we're constantly bombarded with messages that tell us so. If our body doesn't meet the standard, we know that we're valued less. The obligation of meeting the standard, or at least trying to, is called appearance-related social pressure.

Not everyone suffers the same degree of pressure. People read as women suffer much more because they're conceived of as objects of desire, and physical attractiveness is one of the main values they are recognized for. People read as men are conceived of as subjects of desire, and valued for other attributes such as power and money. In this case, your appearance needs to indicate that you have power and money (through accessories, designer clothing, body language, etc.).

The more people you see in the media who look like you, the less pressure you suffer. You need only switch on the TV to verify that there are more old, fat men than old, fat women. In this sense, people of colour suffer even greater pressure, because they are the least represented.

We're pushed to accept our bodies but only to the extent that they look as they 'should'. If they don't, we have to at least make an effort. Make-up, plastic surgery, diets, products to clear the skin, hair removal, hair-straightening treatments ... With the boom in image-enhancing technology, we've reached the point where even the people who work as models in advertising don't resemble the photographs that make them popular; retouching is the order of the day and spectacular videos of the process can be found on social media. Despite knowing this, we all feel the pressure to look like these models, as well as guilt for not being as tall, as thin, as white.

The body, which could be the temple of pleasure, becomes an enemy that we subject to all kinds of tortures on the path to reaching an unattainable goal.

Accept your body because it's beautiful

In the face of so much violence against such an important part of a person, various movements defending the body have emerged. One movement with many followers is called *body positivity*. If the main instruction to us is 'Accept your body only if it's beautiful', the movement in favour of body positivity changes it to 'Accept your body *because* it's beautiful' and puts forth the idea that all bodies are good-looking 'in their own way'. It encourages us to see unconventional beauty where we would previously have seen ugliness. However, even though this philosophy is less violent to the body, it doesn't separate us from the obligation to be beautiful. Dieting is no longer required, because there's also beauty in fat bodies. Straightening our hair is no longer required, because it's also pretty when curly. But even if it's in a much broader and more individual way, body positivity is still about upholding a kind of beauty.

Aesthetic activism

Aesthetic activism can have a very important anti-racist component, as shown by the many Afro-descendant activists working

to increase the visibility of a wider variety of Black female models and working against the hyper-sexualization they often experience. Desirée Bela-Lobedde, whose book *Ser mujer negra en España* [Being a Black Woman in Spain] was published in Spain a few years ago, talks about the racist mechanisms woven into the hegemonic system of beauty while offering advice for better upkeep of Black hair and Afros on social media. Where pressure on appearance and racism intersect, it's no longer a question of only accepting certain bodies as desirable and others as less so, but also about denying the humanity of all the people outside whiteness.

Accept your body because it is

The movement for *body neutrality* goes a little further than body positivity, and states that the beauty of our nose is as important as the beauty of our liver. That is, not very. Instead of encouraging us to love our bodies because they are beautiful, whatever they look like, it encourages us to accept our bodies because they are ours and to value ourselves by other parameters. Body neutrality doesn't deny that beauty might have some importance, but does remove it from the centre of our concerns. Rather than increasing the number of possible kinds of beauty in our society, it proposes minimizing the value we place on beauty in general.

The body neutrality movement argues that personal value doesn't depend on physical attractiveness and is only one of the thousand aspects that make a person. Appearances change continuously throughout life (and throughout the day!): there are times we like our looks more, times not so much, and that's fine. The idea is to get to a place where our happiness doesn't depend on our physical appearance. We must eliminate physical attractiveness as an essential condition for happiness and recognize that, on the contrary, worrying about physical attractiveness is an obstacle to happiness.

To me this seems a very reasonable life philosophy. There is only one tiny problem: it goes against everything we've been taught about how the world works, and unlearning this isn't straightforward. With an eye to future generations, we can stop telling little ones that they're pretty as the go-to praise and congratulate them for other reasons; we can stop making disparaging comments about our bodies; we can show our pride in successes that go beyond having blue eyes or the waistline of a film star.

'Beauty' on show

The importance of beauty doesn't stop at oneself: having a conventionally attractive partner is also a factor in social prestige. So men, who don't suffer so much pressure in relation to their appearance, suffer greater pressure to have a beautiful girlfriend. They often offload this pressure onto their partners, then try to control their appearance. In a 2008 study, Sue Wilkinson explains that heterosexual women who don't shave their legs are pressured by their partners to do so, but only when their legs will be on show. The women interviewed explained that their partners don't want their friends to see them unshaven, because they would be embarrassed by having a hairy girlfriend. That is, even though the majority of men don't care whether their partner shaves or not, public exposure of body hair is a step too far. The issue is no longer whether the man likes the woman in question, but that her image be publicly 'acceptable'.

This should make us think about our own desires. Have you ever liked a person but discounted them as a romantic and sexual partner because they wouldn't be accepted in your circle? Are you sure you like the kind of person that you like, or maybe it seems that you like the kind of person you think you should? How would you feel if someone who matters to you laughed at a person you have a romantic and sexual relationship with because of their physical appearance? What would you do?

Desire with the five senses

Up to now we've discussed superficial attractiveness, as if it's the only kind that exists. Of course, there's also having an attractive personality, but we're not getting into that. Sticking to the body, we can go beyond sight and recognize that sometimes we're attracted to a person we don't know, whom we might not even rate as very good-looking, but who has that something we're drawn to.

Smell is a sense that plays an important role in who we like. It's very difficult to feel attracted to someone whose smell bothers you, however typically attractive their physique may be. In fact, there are various studies that corroborate how finding another person's smell pleasant is a key factor in the success of a romantic–sexual relationship. When we talk about smell, we don't mean an odour modified by deodorants and perfumes (which can either help or hinder) but the smell our bodies really give off. It's not clear why we like how some people smell and not others, but it's an undeniable fact. The smell of genitals can be a very potent aphrodisiac – and a big turn-off too.

When we come to physical contact, touch is clearly essential, and here we have a whole world to explore, because beyond the (quite unreal) clichés of smooth, shaven legs, the body offers textures, densities and volumes that are more difficult to stereotype and advertise. With eyes closed (or blindfolded), we can experiment with what arouses us, and this can be a first step away from the aesthetic education that we've endured. What parts of the other person do we like to touch, embrace, kiss, lick, bite? Where does being touched, embraced, kissed, licked, bitten turn us on?

Dissident bodies

Even though appearance-related pressure affects everyone and can have devastating effects on self-esteem, certain bodies are especially vulnerable. The idea that there are *correct* bodies, and therefore others that are *wrong*, affects all humankind, but if you have all the body parts you're supposed to, even if they are not the *correct* shape, you're already at an advantage.

Having all the parts of the body you 'should have' (and not having any you shouldn't) means many things. It means having two legs, two arms, two eyes, two ears, and these legs, these arms, these eyes, these ears functioning in the standard way.

And, of course, if you're in the 'woman' box, you have prominent breasts and a vulva, and if you're in the 'man' box, you have a penis and testicles.

Having a dissident body means disappearing from the list of desirable bodies, and therefore the idea that these undesirable bodies could have a sexual life is unimaginable. People who use a wheelchair, fat people, people with achrondoplasia, and all the extremely long list of others that cross your mind right now aren't seen as desirable, and their desire is belittled. It seems ridiculous to 'normal' people that they could take pleasure in a body socially considered misshapen. This ridicule is extended to ageism, especially in the case of older women, where the assumption is that they shouldn't have a sex life once they're no longer fertile.

Objectification of dissidence

In parallel with rejecting the idea that bodies considered less than beautiful can enjoy sexuality and share desire and pleasure with other bodies (especially if they share them with normative bodies) is a fetishization of the 'defect'. Any commercial pornography site has sections in which 'standard' bodies are normalized, and non-conventional bodies are exoticized, in the style of the freak shows of bygone eras. There we also find categories of common 'deviations', such as 'hairy lesbians' or 'old people'.

Denying the possibility of desire and pleasure to specific people, while simultaneously exploiting them as part of the sexual fantasies of those with normalized bodies, is a doubly cruel way of dehumanizing them. There are collectives which counter all this and fight for the visibility and recognition of people with non-normative bodies as exactly what they are: people.

More possibilities, more freedom

As happens in so many other spheres, people who don't fit the norm seek strategies to handle the void of references which usually have positive repercussions for everyone. In the same way that non-heterosexual people necessarily have to expand their practices beyond penis/vagina intercourse, thereby enriching the palette of options for everyone, people with disabilities remain excluded from the archetypes of dominant desire and find themselves pushed to investigate beyond any established script. Far outside the norm, they can develop practices that point to less travelled, yet equally satisfying, paths that increase potential pleasure for everyone.

In the documentary directed by Antonio Centeno and Raúl de la Morena called *Yes, We Fuck!*, we see people with non-normative bodies talking about their sexuality and showing it off. The directors explain that they made the film aiming to make visible a reality that is systematically denied. Since the film was made, there have been photography exhibitions, academic conferences and many other pretexts to meet up and discuss what a large part of society doesn't want to see.

Transformation

Appearance-related pressures force people to do everything possible to get closer to the norm. They're not easy to escape, even when we know for sure that we'll never reach certain aspects of the norm, and the temptation to compensate with the parts of our physique that we can indeed 'improve' is very strong. Physical appearance as a project requiring constant attention that hasn't yet reached perfection, or has already passed its peak, is an unquestionable source of frustration and dissatisfaction, not least because ageing is inevitable, and old age doesn't match the standards of what is desirable.

I don't mean by all this that I don't understand (and share) the urge to look attractive, or that there aren't special occasions when I make an effort to 'look good'. What I mean is that 'looking good' cannot be the centre of life, because the expectations are unattainable and there's always some detail that doesn't quite fit. Being a person with a body considered more or less 'acceptable' makes it easier for me to say this than if my body were far from being so. Luckily, many other people of all sizes, all shapes, all colours also state this, as browsing the #bodyneutral hashtag on social media will confirm.

We transform our bodies in many ways. Some are dictates of gender (removing hair or wearing high heels if you're a woman, wearing your hair short if you're a man), others are more or less free personal choices within a finite range of possibilities, such as the kind of clothes we wear (as long as we respect mandates of gender). Some people dedicate a large part of their time and energy to sculpting their bodies, in a process that may be a blend of narcissism, insecurity and consumerism, but may also be driven by the desire to be healthy and enjoy their fullest physical potential. However, we demand transformations of some people that go beyond 'optional' ones.

Growing up as a trans person means receiving constant messages that your body is incorrect, not only because when you're wearing clothes you don't look how a person of your gender is supposed to look, but because when you undress your body contradicts all the axioms we've been sold about sex/gender. The idea of 'a woman's brain in a man's body' or 'a man's brain in a woman's body' is a simplified way of understanding the trans reality that some people in the group also adhere to.

Some time ago, there was an ad running on buses in Spain that said 'Boys have a penis, girls have a vulva. Don't be fooled.' Many people were outraged by this transphobic message, but isn't this exactly what we say in schools? Isn't that what all the biology books say? Haven't we seen thousands of books about sex education with two contrasting drawings, in one of which is a boy with a penis, and in the other a girl with a vulva? So if your body is that of a 'girl', but your gender identity is 'boy', there's been an error that needs to be corrected.

We have a deeply rooted idea that the penis is what makes a person a man. If you have one, you're a man; if you don't have one, you're not. The vulva doesn't count for much, because culturally it's been seen as the absence of a penis rather than a presence in itself, and is often represented as a hole and no more.

This generalized transphobia leads some trans people to have a troubled relationship with their bodies in general, and with genitals and breasts in particular, and this can affect sexual relationships. The solution to discomfort with the body (of any kind) suggested by society is to change it, and there are more options for doing so now than there were a few years ago. In addition to various, increasingly realistic binders and prostheses, hormone therapy and surgery are potential means of body transformation (if you have the resources to access them) and they make the lives of many trans people easier.

Looking like a cis person when trans is called passing – that is, when 'no one notices' that a person is trans – and passing leads to suffering less discrimination. But what about the people who can't or don't want to pass?

In his book *The Myth of the Wrong Body*, Miquel Missé talks about how body transformations are offered as a personal solution to a social problem – the problem being the rigidity of the rules regulating bodies. There are no wrong bodies: there are oppressive rules and unrealistic ideas about how bodies really are. Many people find themselves living at odds with social norms in an exhausting resistance, when in theory social norms should help us to live better. A system that excludes the vast majority of the population and makes life impossible for a significant part of it is an absurd system that needs to be abolished or – at least – modified.

There are no bodies or brains of one gender or the other, but there are norms that make us believe that there is only one possible body if you're a woman, and another if you're a man. The error doesn't lie in bodies or identities; the error is in the system which makes a simplistic construction pass for reality.

Beyond awareness

Knowing that the problem isn't our bodies, but a system that persuades us that our bodies are a problem, doesn't free us from the feelings of inadequacy that have been forged over years of indoctrination and discrimination. Hearing someone close to you talking about their body has a strange effect. In general, they'll find it much more ugly than the rest of us do. How would we talk about our bodies if they belonged to someone else? Would we abuse them as much? Or, to put it another

way: why do we judge bodies so harshly in general? Are they the highest priority in our human relationships?

Overcoming the hostility we feel towards our own bodies (and towards those of others) is a necessary step towards fully enjoying them. It's very difficult to focus on desire and pleasure if we feel uncomfortable in our skin, we feel ashamed of displaying our bodies or we believe that some of our features make us undesirable. Transforming certain aspects of our physique can help to overcome hostility, and we should do so if it will help us to live better, but this can't be the only strategy that we use. Combining it with questioning the stereotypes of hegemonic beauty, and activism for the elimination of pressures related to appearance generally, will help us feel better – if not in our bodies, at least in our lives.

Re-educating taste

You might honestly think: 'I like people with normative physiques – I can't help it. I don't have anything against people who don't have normative physiques, but I'm not attracted to them.' Although you consciously think that this is the case, it's possible that you've had sexual and emotional relationships with people who aren't so normative, or been attracted to them. Maybe you don't realize that you could be attracted to other types of people because you think it impossible. Opening yourself up to this possibility is the first step towards it happening.

When we talk about beauty, we're actually talking about the expectations created about how bodies should be, not bodies as they actually are. Eliminating expectations helps us to enjoy bodies as they are. Eliminating expectations means accepting that my body is as it is, and it's fantastic because it allows me to live so many experiences.

But why should you want to re-educate your taste? As I see it, to gain in the same way as when you add a greater variety of practices to the sexual menu, however much you like penis/vagina penetration. Having encounters with a more diverse range of people offers unexplored possibilities of desire and pleasure. Do you really want to miss out?

For a start, it can help to look for examples beyond the hegemonic models. They're not handed to us on a plate, but it's relatively easy to do a little research to find activists for body neutrality or body positivity who can help us to see bodies in a radically different way.

On the other hand, being someone open to stimuli who listens to their body's reactions can also make us understand our responses to people who, in theory, we wouldn't consider desirable. It's difficult to recognize desire when you don't believe it possible, and simpler to recognize it when you believe anything is possible.

With a little luck, on the path to accepting our own bodies we'll learn to value those of others, and vice versa. Not for their beauty or lack of it, but because sharing bodies for a while in pursuit of desire and pleasure is a gift we mutually give one another. What beauty there is in free gestures like these.

~~vibrator~~ toys

An eventful history

It's very possible that if I say olisbos or hand crank you won't know what I'm talking about. They are old words for referring to what today we call a dildo or vibrator. Sex toys have been known by various names throughout history, because even thousands of years ago people were using sex toys (toys from Neolithic times have been discovered) and those with a phallic shape, made from materials that endure through the passage of time, have left the clearest traces.

The usual word in Catalan – *consolador*, or consoler – has slightly worrying connotations. Who does it console? About what? We can assume that it's meant to console women who don't have a penis nearby, and from there comes the idea that sex toys are substitutes for something, something real, and women use them when they don't have access to this real thing used in real sexual encounters.

The taboo about the infinite variety of toys we can use when we have sex with others or when we masturbate surely comes from this: if it's socially accepted that the aim of sexual relations is reproduction and/or men's pleasure, through vagina/penis intercourse, everything used outside this rationale – and purely for pleasure that isn't the male's – is suspect.

It is so suspect that sex shops (curiously named, as if you could buy sex there and not the ingredients for having it) often have dark, shadowy entrances, and the bags in which your purchases are placed are often made of thick, unbranded paper.

Early pocket vibrators were sold commercially as massage appliances for housewives in women's magazines, and advertisements showed them being used on the head, back or legs, always well away from the clitoris, which was in fact the prime goal of the machine. Vibrators had been invented some years before to help psychoanalysts masturbate their patients, in supposed treatment for the supposed illness of hysteria (which years later was proven not to exist).

The reach of shame

The taboos around toys and masturbation provoke attitudes of shame and fear: the shame of openly seeking pleasure – especially if you are a woman – and the fear that your partner might openly seek pleasure beyond what she obtains from interacting with your penis, in the case of cishet men. Some men are bothered by their partner stimulating her clitoris with her hands or toys during intercourse, as if liking anything else is an affront to their masculinity.

According to a 2017 study by the Catalan non-profit organization Sida Studi, 90% of girls between 14 and 16 years of age state that they don't masturbate, while 90% of boys of the same age state that they do. The rate of masturbation is stable in men and remains at 90% throughout life, while in women the percentage rises with age to reach 70%. The Victoria Milán platform did a study in 2018 which asserted that half of women between 46 and 55 years of age masturbated every day. This contradicts the idea that the youngest women are the most sexually active.

For a significant number of women, self-exploration is a taboo that has to be overcome with age, and a significant number of men think that their penis should be the only source of a couple's pleasure. Therefore it's understandable that the use of toys isn't as widespread as would be reasonably expected if we keep in mind the pleasure that they can help achieve.

On the other hand, at many parties (like hen parties), sex toys are used for comic purposes, serving for a laugh in the moment and with no expectation of anything being done with them afterwards. A woman having a dildo or a vibrator is considered a joke, and the woman who carries it in her bag being caught out is a recurring gag in comedies and funny TV programmes. Thus, the possibility of women seeking pleasure beyond intercourse is ridiculed, and the eroticism stripped from the tools with which they could find it.

At the 2018 Consumer Electronic Show, a famous technological trade show in the USA, a state-of-the-art vibrator created by the Lora Dicarlo company, designed to emulate the movements of the mouth while performing oral sex on a vulva, won the innovation award in the drones and robotics category. Even though for years it has been common to have women doing striptease and sex toys dedicated to (cis) men at the trade show, the organization decided to strip the Osé of the award, for being 'immoral, obscene, indecent and profane'. This injustice had such widespread repercussions in the media that the organization had to backtrack and return the award to the company. That is, well into the twenty-first century, there are some who openly say that a sex toy is 'obscene' if it is mostly targeted at women. Luckily, well into the twenty-first century, there is also a feminist movement strong enough to condemn and question this.

Something for everybody

There are all kinds of sex toys. Some are used to directly stimulate the genitals, others are accessories that can be used to stimulate fantasy. The best-known ones are dildos (which have a phallic shape and don't vibrate) and vibrators (which can have various shapes and even a remote control that someone else can activate). The more research that is done on the clitoris, the more the shape of the toys aimed at it changes: they've gone from having phallic shapes for the most part to embracing the labias majora and minora, and seeking different points and intensities of stimulation. Clitoral suction stimulators, which cause more intense sensations, are another kind of vibrator.

There are double dildos for couples to use, if at least one of the two people has a vulva, which allows simultaneous penetration of the two people participating, and also harnesses, which allow a strap-on dildo to vaginally or anally penetrate the other person.

Within the range of penetration, there are also Venus balls, which serve to strengthen the vaginal walls and can be very pleasurable to wear while doing other things. Anal dilators are cone-shaped and can be introduced little by little as the anus dilates, and there are both vibrating and non-vibrating anal plugs too. Anal balls allow for play both when being inserted into the anus and when being removed.

For people who have a penis, there are strokers, which can be tube-shaped for full insertion or egg-shaped for partial insertion. There are also cock rings that tighten around the base of the penis and stimulate blood circulation, which lengthens and intensifies the erection (but not necessarily the pleasure).

There are also nipple clamps, with a wide range of strengths, feathers for caresses, whips for whipping . . .

The best thing to do is to go to a sex shop, with plenty of both time and curiosity. The people working there are usually ready to explain anything required and advise according to the needs and preferences of those who come in, and they also offer items at a wide variety of prices.

Lubricant is an accessory that mustn't be forgotten: many people don't keep it in mind, but it can help make sexual encounters much more pleasant, whatever genitals you have, and it's essential if penetration is planned. Some people believe that lubricant is only necessary for anal penetration, but it's been proven that extra lubrication increases pleasure in both vaginal and anal penetration and in interaction between any part of the body/object and genitals. When we're talking about lubrication, it's always better to have too much than too little.

Although toys can open up possibilities and amplify sensations, it's important to remember that we use them to sharpen desire and gain further pleasure. Focusing more on the accessory than on the sensations we're experiencing is a perfect way of disconnecting from pleasure and ending up feeling that it's not worth it. It must also be remembered that, although trying a toy or a sex game seems like a good idea in theory, if we're not comfortable when we put it on, it's best to stop and do something else.

Home made

Apart from the objects expressly conceived for use during sexual encounters, we also have a whole range of accessories that are designed for other things but that we can make use of just as well – scarves to blindfold us, ties and string as restraints. Food also gives us plenty to play with: from phallic-shaped vegetables of all sizes for penetrating one another, to honey, chocolate or anything sticky that we can lick. The advantage of playing with food is that it's natural, cheaper than sex toys, smells good and usually contributes to hydrating the skin.

Lingerie (or any piece of clothing that turns us on) can also be an interesting accessory, especially if we break free from conventional use and dare ourselves to wear pieces we normally wouldn't or in ways that we normally wouldn't wear them.

Woven fabrics or tactile objects that we can use to caress or cause more intense sensations are another source of stimulation. Bringing cold or warm objects close to certain parts of the body, or varying the intensity of bites and caresses can also be interesting.

If our creativity is awakened, it must be kept very much in mind that when we insert objects into the anus, they must have some sort of flared base which impedes the body completely sucking them in. If this happens (it's more common than you'd think), you must go to hospital. Also avoid inserting any kind of object that could create a vacuum (a bottle, for example) into the vagina or anus, and keep any substance with alcohol (it stings like hell) away from the genitals and anus.

Power to the imagination

A significant part of the pleasure obtained from sexual games comes not from the physical stimuli provoked by the game itself, but from the arousal caused by something new (or something routine that we really like). Aside from accessories, fantasies and role play (with or without costumes) can be very stimulating.

Solo fantasies are surely the most widely used 'sex toy': they don't require consent, they can be turned to at any time and no one else needs to know what we're thinking. It can also be thrilling to share them, and the game can begin long before physical interaction, even at a distance. Telling someone we've arranged to meet a few hours later what we'd like to do can be exciting, as well as serving as a way of negotiating practices and constructing enthusiastic consent.

Fantasies aren't practices or situations we want to experience, they are practices or situations we like to *imagine*: this is an important difference. Sometimes it can be very exciting to imagine certain things which would upset us greatly if they were really to happen. For this reason, we should never take a sexual partner sharing their fantasy as an invitation to carry it out. Before moving from fantasy to acting it out, you need to be sure that the other person wants to try it.

Images, words

Images with sexual content are usually used during masturbation and can also be part of shared sexual encounters. In this book, we've already talked a lot about hegemonic pornography and the problems it presents. Movements of feminist pornography and post-pornography seek to offer alternatives and are worth exploring.

When it comes to home-made pictures, they can be a magnificent tool for taking the reins of your own desire, and daring to imagine erotic situations far removed from stereotypes. Exchanging photographs, voice-notes, videos or text messages with someone we don't have nearby is a way of having long-distance sex, and we can make it even more special if we apply some originality. If we decide to exchange erotic audiovisual material with someone, we must remember that sharing it with third parties without explicit consent is illegal in many countries, as well as showing a lack of respect.

When chemicals come into play

Many people use substances which alter consciousness or perception for experimenting within their sexual encounters. Before using (legal or illegal) drugs in sexual contexts, everyone participating must be clear what the purpose of using them is, and the limits we don't want to go beyond. Personally, I don't recommend using drugs in situations where we are vulnerable (when there are people we don't know or when we're not absolutely sure that the people there will respect us), because they can push us into practices and risks we wouldn't consider if we were in full possession of our faculties.

Knowing what both short-term and long-term consequences drugs could have is essential. There are a great many official organizations with websites where you can find information and even services you can send a sample of a drug for analysis (at an affordable price) so you can be assured that it's unadulterated and really is the drug you think it is.

It's not a good idea to drink alcohol or take other drugs if you're taking medication, because it increases the risk of an overdose or undesirable side effects. Nor is it appropriate to take drugs when you're in a bad mood, or in a depressed or fatigued state, because these emotional states will probably be heightened. If you use drugs as an accessory in sexual encounters, it doesn't make much sense to take them when you don't feel like having sex, which is normal with depression or fatigue. Sleeping well, adequate hydration and eating before and after taking drugs helps the body handle them better.

It's a good idea to think about how you will get home if you end up somewhere else (obviously you can't drive under the influence of drugs), and also a good idea to tell someone you trust, who won't be partaking, when you're taking drugs. This way they can check that you're all right and no one is taking things too far.

Just like having sex, taking drugs is an important decision that must be taken freely, without pressure from anyone. If you're not certain you want to do it, it may be worth waiting until you feel more sure.

And much more

One of the most marvellous aspects of sex is, that despite hegemonic culture, it's totally personal. Every combination of two or more people who share experiences and imaginings is unique. In fact, every new experience – even if it's with people we've had sex with thousands of times – is unique. The possibilities for playing, inventing, exploring are infinite. As with any journey, both the preparations and the memories are part of the enjoyment; it's worth spending time and excitement on them. The anticipation of what we will do is exciting, as is remembering what we've done. Sharing sex and appreciating it are ingredients that improve relationships and contribute to a growing desire for more. Let's make the most of it!

~~sex education~~
care

The sex education classes that a large part of the population receive aren't meant to educate about the reality of people as sexual beings or about the potential for pleasure, but are a kind of instruction about the dangers of having sex, with the condom as a universal saviour. These classes start from all the assumptions we've been disproving, and are even more problematic than the stereotypes that we receive from popular culture, because school is a source of authority.

These classes speak exclusively about heterosexual coitus and are based on two great fears: unwanted pregnancy and sexually transmitted infections (STIs). Even though offering information about how to protect yourself from the possible consequences of sexual activity is appropriate, limiting them to this seems completely insufficient. It's even more serious if we bear in mind that there are no suggestions for protecting yourself from STIs in any practice that isn't penis/vagina intercourse.

If we agree that literature classes are much more effective when a passion for reading is passed on to the young person and when they are offered various good-quality books, how can it be that we have so little desire to bring young people closer to sexual richness and diversity? How can it be that we focus on reinforcing the idea of sexuality as limited and dangerous, instead of presenting it as a fascinating facet of life that can be shared with generosity and joy? It seems that, rather than encouraging the exploration of sexuality, we want quite the opposite.

Given the focus of formal sex education today, it's understandable that the majority of young people turn to other sources for information. Generally, the most used channels are groups of friends, but they also turn to the internet (especially boys) or family (especially girls). Luckily, every day there are more specialist centres with information services for young people, well-prepared material distributed through various channels, and even television programmes, such as *Sex Education* on Netflix, which address sex from an open, detailed perspective.

For a respectful, responsible education about sexuality

When we decide that we want to get a driving licence, we are obviously warned about certain dangers (driving under the influence of alcohol or other drugs or getting distracted at the wheel, for example). But, despite the very high number of traffic accidents, no one tries to dissuade us from driving or limits themselves to explaining how to use a seatbelt or a breathalyser. We are taught the rules of the road, how to be comfortable while driving and to try not to knock anyone down. That is, we are taught to drive in a respectful, responsible way.

This is precisely what I find lacking in the sex education we offer adolescents. Talking about consent, respecting your own rhythms and those of others, listening to desire, trusting the body more than stereotypes. On the other hand, heterocentric and coitocentric education reinforces the discrimination suffered by non-cishet people in secondary schools. It makes out that they don't exist or that, if they do exist, they are an oddity. Not only do they not receive specific information about sexual health, they get the message that their sexuality is inappropriate. The rest of the class also gets this message. This is textbook LGBTphobia and gives rise to even more serious violence that occurs in many educational centres.

According to the organizers of Oasis, a free space aimed at LGBTIQ+ people between twelve and seventeen years old in Catalonia, all the people they work with have been victims of LGBTphobia in schools, and half have suffered physical and sexual attacks. The issue is grave enough to be taken seriously, starting with appropriate teacher training and the establishment of protocols that stop in its tracks discriminatory behaviour by anyone in the school environment.

Are you sure it's safe sex?

The idea that carrying a condom in your pocket will protect you from all possible ills can be reassuring, but it's very dangerous. For a start because, while many people know that using a condom is required, they're not too sure when. Besides, even if there's a penis involved in a sexual encounter, it doesn't automatically follow that it's erect. Is it still 'dangerous' to go near it, when it's not erect? If he doesn't ejaculate, is a condom needed? Using a condom during penis/vagina intercourse, or for part of it, can give a false sense of 'doing it right' and lead to taking on other risky behaviours.

When we have sex, any exchange of fluids can involve transmission of an STI, even kissing on the mouth. It's very difficult (if not impossible) to have sexual encounters without coming into contact with the other person's fluids, and so even so-called safe sex isn't completely safe. However, we can minimize the risks and have safer sexual encounters. Not indulging in reckless acts is especially advisable.

A significant number of fatal accidents happen outside the home, and many are traffic accidents. This doesn't stop us going out onto the streets or using public and private transport. What we do to protect ourselves is recognize risky behaviour and minimize it. We look from side to side before crossing a road, we don't drive if we've been drinking, we wear our seatbelts. When it comes to sexuality, wider information about what risks we run when we decide to participate in certain activities won't save us from anything, but it will help us decide to what point we are willing to take them on. The aim is to strike a balance between prophylactic obsession and reckless neglect, the point at which we freely enjoy what we are doing without putting anyone's health at serious risk.

Take care of others, take care of yourself

Minimizing risk isn't only a show of respect towards the people we have sex with, it's also a show of self-esteem. Although the treatment of STIs has come a long way, some are chronic and

will have lifelong consequences. Studies have shown a certain relaxation about them in recent years, which has led to an increase in cases of syphilis and other serious infections among cis men and the people they have sex with.

Just as practices must be consensual from a perspective of desire, they must also be consensual from a perspective of health, and forethought given to the protection we will use. If we know we have an STI, the most honest thing to do is to explain. This way, the other person can decide what risks they wish to assume, and we take responsibility for trying not to infect anyone.

Informing sexual partners from the past six months when we are diagnosed with an STI may be awkward, but it helps immensely in minimizing the consequences. These people will have the pertinent tests, be treated if necessary, and take responsibility for not infecting anyone else. With some STIs, rapid detection is key to avoiding serious after-effects.

Trust is not enough

Many people think that there's no need to protect themselves from STIs when having sex with their stable partner, especially if they have a pact of monogamy. Unfortunately, experience shows that people don't always stick to pacts. Again, the level of communication we have with the other person can indicate how far we can risk trusting them.

In any case, if you have an active sexual life, it's a good idea to get tested for STIs at least once a year. If the person who normally sees us in the medical centre makes it awkward, there are walk-in sexual health clinics where confidential, discreet tests are done. Getting tested doesn't help to prevent anything, but it is a simple, non-invasive way of reassuring us that everything is fine, and allows us to take measures if there is a problem.

Long live plastic!

Penetration (vaginal, anal or oral with body parts or objects) is the sexual practice with the highest risk of STI transmission and so the message that condoms are valuable is a good one, but not only in heterosexual intercourse. If we penetrate with our hands, we can use latex (or vinyl, if any person involved is allergic to latex) gloves. This is especially important if we have cuts on our hands. The gloves can be used as protection during any contact between the hands and the genitals or anus, and they are easy to find in supermarkets.

If we penetrate with phallic-shaped objects or with the penis, we can use condoms. The condom should be used during the entire contact, not only before ejaculation, and it must be changed if it's been on for a while (as a guide, every fifteen minutes). If we share sex toys, the condom must be changed every time the person using it changes, in the same way that if the same penis penetrates different mouths/vaginas/anuses, the condom must also be changed.

When it comes to oral sex, if we practise it on a penis we can use a condom, and if we practise it on a vulva or anus we have various options. The most usual is cutting off the tip of the condom and opening out the cylinder so we're left with a rectangle that we can place on the vulva or anus. In pharmacies and sex shops, we can find female condoms or dental dams, which are rectangles of latex specifically meant for performing oral sex on vulvas or anuses. In a pinch, we can also use cling film, but we must ensure that it's not perforated.

A high percentage of cis men declare that they don't like putting on condoms because 'it's too small' and 'too tight'. Condoms being too small for so many cis men is statistically impossible: latex is a very elastic material which fits well and works for the vast majority of penises. It needs to be a little tight to avoid fluids entering or coming out of it, as this is precisely what protects against STIs and pregnancies. There are special condoms which are a little bit bigger for exceptional cases in which the standard ones really are too small, but using a larger size than required drastically reduces effectiveness.

Many cis men also try to delay the moment of putting on the condom or don't put one on at all because 'You don't feel anything with a condom.' It's a pity that they have this limited perception of sexuality, but in any case the risks of not using one are high enough to make this a lame excuse. If you don't feel like using a condom, you can stick to less risky practices than (vaginal, oral or anal) penetration, such as masturbation, long-distance sex or caresses without exchange of fluids.

When a person tries to cross the line of what we think is acceptable when it comes to assumable risks, it is a clear sign that we should maximize precautions: if they're trying this with me, they've probably tried it with other sexual partners and therefore it's possible they are a person who habitually engages in risky practices without protection.

Prophylactic aggression or *stealthing* is the name for the act of removing the condom during penetration or just beforehand without the other person's consent, and as well as being a dangerous and disrespectful act, it's considered sexual assault and can be reported.

Let's watch out for wounds!

A person having lesions or open wounds in the genital/anal area can be a sign of certain STIs – such as genital herpes, warts or syphilis – that are passed on by contact with these wounds. In these cases, it's even more advisable to use barrier methods (condoms, dental dams, gloves).

Abundant use of lubricant reduces the likelihood of small cuts that can happen during vaginal or anal penetration, and therefore also contributes to safer sexual practices.

And contraception?

Contraception being left until last is due to the fact that information about this is what we usually have most readily available. It's difficult to live in today's society and not be aware of the most widespread contraceptive methods, which are condoms and hormonal contraception.

If we decide on hormonal contraception, the medium- and long-term effects it has on health have to be kept in mind. The consumption of oestrogens and progesterone can cause depression, mood swings and decreased libido. It's quite the contradiction that medication we use to enjoy sexuality without fear of pregnancy has a side effect of decreasing interest in sex, but that's how it is.

It must be remembered that, other than barrier methods, contraceptives don't protect against STIs. All in all, it's worth using a barrier method and protecting yourself from everything with a single method of contraception.

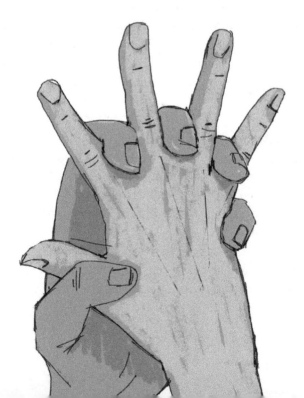

When choosing methods of contraception, the most important thing is to seek professional advice that shows us all the options and helps us choose the most suitable one for our circumstances. Since people with uteruses are the ones who run the risk of pregnancy and will inevitably have to bear the consequences, they must be the ones to decide what makes them feel safest and most comfortable, and this isn't up for negotiation. There is a myth that trans men who take hormonal treatment in the form of testosterone and don't have a period can't get pregnant. This is false, because they may ovulate even though they don't have periods, and there are more cases of accidental pregnancy in this group than you might expect.

Emergency contraception is a tablet that must be taken within seventy-two hours of intercourse, and it's exactly what the name suggests: an emergency method that must be used if, for some reason, other methods have failed. It can't be taken as a regular contraceptive because it alters the menstrual cycle and its effectiveness can decrease, besides the health side effects for the person taking it. In the UK, it's free and can be obtained from sexual health clinics and GP surgeries. It can also be purchased without a prescription at pharmacies.

Legislation on abortion depends on where you live. There is currently a significant offensive by the far right against the rights of women (and any person able to gestate) regarding their own bodies, but there are also organized movements lobbying for more egalitarian legislation.

If you find yourself in need of an abortion and don't know your rights, you can look for the nearest support group, or approach a feminist collective that can help you obtain information. You don't need to go through this difficult situation alone – there are lots of people ready to help you.

Don't lose sight of the joy of fucking!
After all this, having sex and protecting your health at the same time may seem complicated, but it really isn't a big deal. Protective measures can often be included within the game of sex, and we can play them down by looking at the funny side. Besides, the awareness that taking care of your own health and that of others is a loving gesture contributes to healthier, fuller and freer sexual encounters. Long live safer sex!

~~love~~
affection

Sexuality's revolutionary potential soon emerges when we recognize it as an inexhaustible source of free pleasure we can explore by ourselves or in a group, through which we can bestow sensations as intense as those from drugs and possibly minimize the risks of unwanted side effects.

The repression of the revolution

Perhaps this revolutionary potential is why oppressive cultures are obsessed with regulating, limiting and ordering sex. Making us fear it, see it as something dangerous and forbidden that must be controlled. That is, robbing sexuality of pleasure as a main objective and adding social functions to it. Attention is deflected from what gives meaning to sexual activities – the pursuit of mutual pleasure based on mutual desire (when we don't practise them alone) – and the emphasis is placed on what is no more than a possible side effect – that is, reproduction. Even though the vast majority of sexual encounters we have don't lead to pregnancy, and even fewer end in giving birth to an infant, our culture has managed to make this possible consequence the only reason for the existence of sex, to the point that some people find pleasure and desire secondary and expendable. Not too long ago, it was considered unacceptable for women to feel pleasure during sex, and in fact, even now, they are asked in a thousand ways to hide their desire.

Rape has also been (and unfortunately still is) used as a weapon of war, and a tool to 'correct' 'deviant' desire. When sexists declare that a woman is a lesbian because she hasn't sampled a 'good dick', they're drawing from this exact idea, just as they want feminists to be raped, or when they say a woman is so ugly no one would want to rape her (they assume that being raped is more desirable than being ugly).

Confusing sexual violence with sexuality is like confusing a punch with a caress. It may concern the same body parts, but the intention, experience and effect have nothing in common. Oppressive cultures succeed in making us grow up to fear sexuality by injecting us with the fear of sexual violence, stripping sexuality of pleasure and desire, and centring reproduction, when in practice it's incidental.

Pure love, dirty sex

Another totally different yet equally effective way of limiting the possibilities of enjoying sex is to mythologize it, make it sacred, grant it almost magical powers. The same romantic comedies that teach us that heterosexual coitus is the only 'real' sexual practice persuade us that the 'true' sex, the best sex, is between two people (only two, preferably heterosexuals and, without any shred of doubt, monogamous) who love one another. Two people who love one another in coupledom, with a kind of Disney love that strikes at first sight, weathers a few difficulties and lives happily ever after.

At the other extreme we have hook-up sex, which is presented as sordid and inferior to 'true' sex. Sex for which the price must be paid, if it doesn't end in a fairytale Disney love and become first-rate sex.

The punishment for casual sex contrasts with the hyper-sexualization seen in the majority of public spheres, which offers us quick, no-strings pleasure. That is, we live with both the idealization of sex when it's about finding a future partner and the trivialization of sexual encounters with people we establish other links with.

Short-lived balance

If we pause for a moment on the idea of a future partner, there's another significant stereotype: stable partners end up abandoning sexuality because desire inevitably fades, and once a certain point is reached, it can only be found outside the couple and 'forces' 'serial' monogamy. So, a pattern of relationships is established in which, like monkeys, people let go of one branch when they have another one to cling to, where it's understood that advancing requires moving from one branch to another. Only temporarily can you have two at the same time.

Banishing pleasure from stable relationships, and at the same time stripping affection from casual sexual encounters, makes us fall into sexualities of consumption, where love and desire are together only for a brief time, at the beginning of the relationship, and where a relationship must be broken off to have another, more exciting one. I refuse to accept this gross simplification of the infinite human possibilities to love enjoyment and to enjoy loving. I demand a life in which it's possible to retain the adventure of exploring desire and pleasure with the people you have long-term relationships with, and also to treat the people you casually explore pleasure with affectionately and respectfully: a revolution of chosen affection against the tyranny of one-size-fits-all relationships.

Anti-capitalist desire?

Casual relationships don't necessarily have to be cold and starved of affection. In fact, the more communication there is, the greater the possibility of them being satisfying for all the people involved. It seems logical to think that respect and closeness should play a part if you're sharing desire and pleasure with someone. Meeting a person and immediately going to bed with them needn't mean treating them like an object, even though popular culture says that it does. Also, being concerned about whether the other person is comfortable and having a good time is a good way of ensuring that they're also concerned about whether we're comfortable and having a good time. For me, the principle of reciprocity is the most desirable thing in any encounter.

On the other hand, I find absurd the very widespread idea that long-term relationships end up being sexually boring. If you know someone well, you feel more confident and more secure to explore more risky practices or ones you're not sure you'll want to see through to the end.

The trivialization of casual encounters and desexualization of long-term relationships are two sides of the same commercialization of sexual relations. In both cases we're led to centre ourselves in selfish, conventional desire without considering the other person as a living being who also desires and evolves and changes – someone whom I can talk to and move forward with and negotiate with. Someone who can uncover aspects of me I don't know myself, and who deserves respect and attention.

So, we're presented with two unrealistic and, to my way of thinking, undesirable extremes: sex without love or love without sex. This isn't how it works in my circle; there is a palette of almost infinite possibilities that every person negotiates the best they can, in the absence of more abundant models of happy sexualities and love.

Inventing possible spaces

Compulsory monogamy has been questioned for many years, and other forms of romantic and sexual relationships have been proposed, so far without the magic formula that will help us live more comfortably and more happily in relationships with the rest of humankind. This is almost certainly because we can't shake off unrealistic expectations: whether it's a conventional relationship or not, we often let the projection of what we would like (or what we believe we should like) cloud our view of what it really is.

What we have learned from unconventional relationships is to question everything. The fewer things we take for granted when we begin a relationship of any kind, the more we talk to the other person or people about how we want to relate to each other (or how we can relate to each other), about our ambitions and our limitations, about what makes us feel good and what

we want to explore, the easier it is for us to feel liberated in what we're doing. There is no insurance against suffering, but we can at least keep talking about how we feel and try to modify wherever necessary to minimize it.

In this regard, very important work is being done by feminists who devote themselves to dismantling the dictates of romantic love. Nowadays, more and more people are rejecting the idea of the other half, of love at first sight, of giving everything and enduring everything for love. If it hurts, tell them it hurts, and if they don't make any attempt to stop hurting you, they don't love you. Or at least, they don't love you well. Sometimes walking away is the only thing that can be done to avoid being hurt, and ending a painful relationship can be a form of love. So can transforming it so that everyone feels good, if possible.

The notion that there is one great love of your life, that this great love is the only important one, that it will last 'forever' and that if it hasn't lasted 'forever' it wasn't good, is very childish. Recognizing the possibility of loving various people, each one in their own way, simultaneously or not, is recognizing a reality closer to the experiences the majority of us have than a Prince Charming or Cinderella waiting for us at some point in our lives with the key to our happiness in their pocket. Establishing how we achieve this is a way of preventing unnecessary pain.

Blah, blah, blah, yeah, yeah, yeah

If telepathy doesn't exist in sex, it doesn't in affection either. When we begin a relationship with someone, it's not enough to put a label on it (lovers, a couple, friends with benefits). In fact, if we don't give it meaning, the label can do more harm than good. How much space do we need? How much attention would we like from the other person? How much can we offer them? Do we want them to be part of our inner circle? Do we want to spend a large part of our free time with them? Do we want to continue having romantic and sexual relationships with other people? Will we be upset if this person does? What are the lines we don't cross? What is non-negotiable for us?

The answers to these questions can end up sketching out a very conventional relationship or one totally different to what we'd previously imagined. If we give ourselves the space to really listen to each other, the key question isn't the kind of relationship we build but on what foundations we build this relationship. Building it on assumptions leads to misunderstandings and disappointment, building it on dialogue and honesty leads to reciprocity and potential for understanding. Talking about how we feel is no guarantee of success, but not talking is usually a guarantee of failure.

Talking about relationships in terms of success and failure is strange, but for me a successful relationship isn't the one that lasts longest, as we've been given to understand, but the one that allows those involved to enjoy it to its fullest. I'm not talking about fun like a funfair, I'm talking about enjoying in the sense of comfort, trust, security, respect. We can't prevent the (emotional, sexual, life) interests we had in common with a person from changing and no longer being shared, but we can try to avoid causing unnecessary suffering. The pain caused by realizing that feelings are no longer requited is inevitable, but if this lack of reciprocity is explained respectfully it may be easier to bear.

Understanding the limits of the possible
Love is infinite, and this is shown by the fact that we usually have several people that we love in our lives. The fact that we make a new friend and come to love them doesn't mean we stop loving the friends we've had before, nor the other people we love in other ways. So why must a romantic relationship erase the others, past and present?

What is clear is that time is limited. The time we spend with someone is usually a good measure of this person's importance in our lives: we spend more time with the people who matter most to us, we make more of an effort to see them and pass up other activities to be with them. This involves a hierarchy – if not of love, at least of the energy we devote to each person. The time we devote to someone can be physical (being with them for a while) or mental (spending a while thinking about that person), and when we meet someone we find exciting we usually devote lots of mental time to them. A good indication that we like someone is the amount of time we spend wanting to be with that person, whether we are or not. A good indication that it's not going well is if, most of the time we spend with someone, we'd like to be somewhere else.

This somewhere might be real or imaginary. 'When X happens, we'll be fine' is a recurring thought of people maintaining an unsatisfactory or even painful relationship. If, when you're with someone, you'd like to be with them, yet not here and now but in other circumstances that perhaps aren't realistic, maybe you don't want to be with this person, but with the idea of them you've created, and the more you know them, the clearer it becomes that this idea doesn't match up to the reality. Again, talking about it can ease the confrontation between fantasy and reality.

Me too, me neither
The best thing that can happen when people get together is that the situation is mutual. Communication can help us to know whether hopes, energies and wishes are shared, but it also helps us modulate our emotional responses. If we want to spend lots of time with a person who wants to see us, but not too often, we can adjust to this with less frustration than might be caused if we don't talk about it, and every five times we suggest hanging

out, the other person accepts only once. At least we know what to expect. It must also be kept in mind that communication isn't only verbal: we know perfectly well that what's said and what's done don't always align. So, if words don't chime with actions, it's better to believe the actions.

Redefining affection

When I suggest talking about affection rather than love, it's because we've emptied the word 'love' of so much that it needs refilling. I mean looking each other in the eye and not saying what we think we're expected to say, but how we truly feel. What are we talking about when we talk about love? Do we need to love a person to respect them and want them to be as comfortable as possible? To what point can we share desire and pleasure with someone we don't like in the least? What do we mean when we say 'I love you'? Why do we say it when we don't feel it at all, and why do we hold back from saying it when we feel it deep inside? What are we afraid of?

One of the fears may be rejection. If I say how I feel and it's not mutual, I have to accept it. If I act on assumptions but don't say anything explicitly, I can always say the other person hasn't interpreted me correctly. This is a catastrophic strategy for two reasons: firstly, because assumptions rapidly become misunderstandings, and if no one clearly says what they feel and what they want, everyone acts amid the uncertainty of whether they are correctly interpreting signals. The second reason is that handling rejection in a society like ours, where it's supposed to be one of the worst things that can happen to you, takes a certain amount of practice that can only be gained by exposure to it. The fewer times you expose yourself to it, the fewer times you'll be explicitly rejected, even though implicit rejection can make you feel equally bad. De-mystifying rejection is as important as de-mystifying romantic love when it comes to building healthy relationships. The more times we're kindly told no, the more times we're respectfully told no, the clearer it will be to us that the fact that another person doesn't want the same thing we do doesn't say anything bad about anyone. There is simply no overlap.

Ideally, if we strip ourselves of expectations and mandates, if we learn to say yes and no without fear, we could share the source of free, inexhaustible pleasure that sexuality can be. But for this to happen, using sexuality as a tool of power, control and suppression must stop, on both the collective and personal levels. That would indeed be a real revolution.

~~end~~ horizon

This book wants to be a book that truly begins as it ends. It hopes that seeds of doubt have been sown, which will blossom into long conversations with people you love, that you are interested in, that you like to mull things over with.

This is a book that considers itself in a state of flux and expects questioning and criticism, a book written as someone thinking out loud because they need to share possible paths. Many people – some without knowing – have participated. All the people with whom I've shared desire and pleasure (to whom I'm sincerely grateful), and all the people who have come on to me, not bothering about my desire, imposing their pleasure, not wanting to share anything. Friends who have explained how they feel and what worries them; the colleagues who have said, 'Look at this, you'll find things here.'

Now it has ended, the book wants to look farther, at the horizon. We have a long way to go to reach a world in which sexualities can be lived freely. Here and now, thousands of people suffer sexual violence. We're penalized for leaving the beaten track – exactly what this book invites us to do. Because the farther we move away from the suffocating norm, the easier everyone will be able to breathe.

Until we get there – to that shining azure horizon, we'll be building. We have more powerful tools to imagine it: desire and pleasure, there for us if we want them. At a time when sexual dissidence is punished, when a body's way of living is commercialized and ordered and imposed on it, loving and being loved, desiring and being desired, enjoying and being enjoyed is a beautiful form of rebellion. Wanna be part of it?

Appendix

How d'you wanna fuck?
This list can help you share your desires with others. The possible activities are endless, so those below are merely inspiration for you to make a list as long as you like. The idea is to share it with the people you want to have sex with, then compare to see which activities you overlap in. Have lots of fun!

	No way!	We could try it	I'm dying to do it!
Giving sensual massages			
Receiving sensual massages			
Doing a striptease			
Having someone do a striptease for you			
Recording yourself while having sex			
Having sex in front of a mirror			

	No way!	We could try it	I'm dying to do it!
Shaving the other person's genitals			
Having the other person shave your genitals			
Watching porn together			
Having sex during a period			
Talking 'dirty'			
Role play with costumes			
Using sex toys			
Playing with candles			
Having sex outside			
Having sex at work			
Watching other people having sex			
Letting others watch you having sex			
Having a threesome			
Having group sex			
Watching your partner do it with someone else			
Having your partner watch you do it with someone else			